Eyewitness
PLANT

Blackberries

Red ginseng root

Gerbera
flower

Moss on
decaying wood

Radish

Peppers

Ornamental
dried corn

Ribwort
plantain
seed heads

Opium poppy
seed heads

Redshank
flowers

Delphinium
flowers

Eyewitness
PLANT

Garden
pansies

In association with
THE NATURAL HISTORY MUSEUM and
THE ROYAL BOTANIC GARDENS, KEW

Written by
DAVID BURNIE

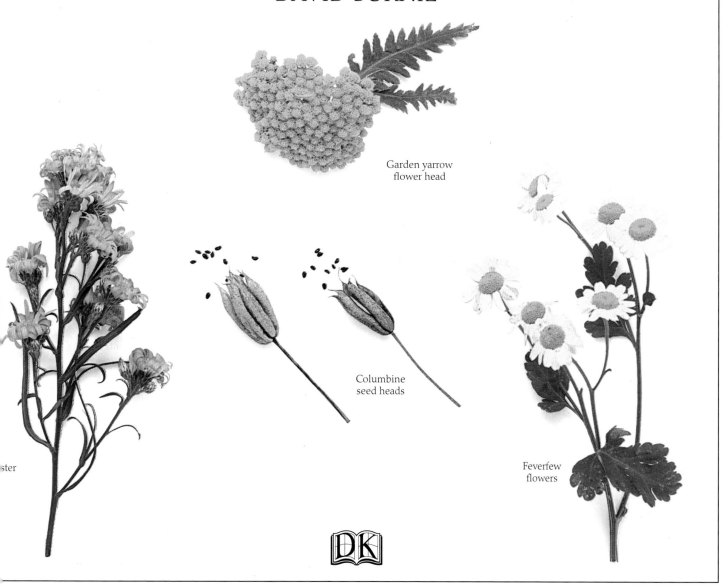

Garden yarrow
flower head

ster

Columbine
seed heads

Feverfew
flowers

DK

Ripe fig cut
in half

Poppy
seed
head

Eucalyptus
leaves

Field
scabiou

Common sorrel

DK

LONDON, NEW YORK,
MELBOURNE, MUNICH, and DELHI

Project editor Helen Parker
Senior editor Sophie Mitchell
Senior art editor Julia Harris
Managing editor Sue Unstead
Managing art editor Roger Priddy
Special photography
Andrew McRobb of the Royal Botanic Gardens, Kew
Jane Burton, Karl Shone, and Kim Taylor
Editorial consultants
The staff of the Natural History Museum, London
and the Royal Botanic Gardens, Kew

Creeping
buttercup

Yarrow
leaf

THIS EDITION
Editors Karen O'Brien, Steve Setford, Jessamy Wood
Art editors Ann Cannings, Peter Radcliffe
Managing editor Julie Ferris, Jane Yorke
Managing art editors Owen Peyton Jones, Jane Thomas
Art director Martin Wilson
Associate publisher Andrew Macintyre
Picture researchers Lorna Ainger, Angela Jones, Harriet Mills
Production editors Jenny Jacoby, Hitesh Patel, Marc Staples
DTP designer Siu Yin Ho
Jacket editor Adam Powley

This Eyewitness ® Guide has been conceived by
Dorling Kindersley Limited and Editions Gallimard

First published in Great Britain in 1989.
This revised edition published in Great Britain in 2011 by
Dorling Kindersley Limited,
80 Strand, London WC2R ORL

Tufted
vetch

2 4 6 8 10 9 7 5 1

175433 – 11/10

A CIP catalogue record for this book is
available from the British Library.

ISBN 978-1-40534-548-4

Colour reproduction by Colourscan,
Singapore; MDP, UK

Printed and bound by Toppan Printing Co.,
(Shenzhen) Ltd, China

Ox-eye
daisy

Common
toadflax

Discover more at
www.dk.com

Spear
thistle

Lords-
and-
ladies

Flower
of blue
echeveria

Contents

Bladder senna   Young peas in pod

What is a plant?

PLANTS ARE THE KEY to life on Earth. Without them, a whole host of other organisms would soon disappear. This is because many living things depend on plants for food and for somewhere to live. Plants are different, because they make food themselves, using energy that they collect from sunlight. There are two main kinds of plant. The simplest ones do not have flowers. They include mosses, liverworts, ferns, and also conifers – the biggest plants that have ever existed on Earth. Compared to them, flowering plants are newcomers, but they have become a huge success. Today, there are about a quarter of a million different kinds of flowering plant, and they grow almost everywhere, from mountain tops to deserts. This book tells their story.

THIS IS NOT A PLANT
It is often difficult to tell simple plants and animals apart. This plant-like organism is a hydrozoan and lives in the sea. Its branches are formed by tiny animals called polyps, which have tentacles to trap particles of food.

Lichen

ALL MIXED UP
A lichen is made up of two different organisms: a tiny non-flowering plant called an alga, and a fungus. The algal cells live among the tiny threads formed by the fungus and supply the fungus with food, which they make using sunlight (pp.14–15). The fungus cannot make its own food and would die without the alga. Lichens grow very slowly and are extremely long-lived.

Lichens growing on limestone roc

THIS WAS A PLANT
Forests of horsetails and giant club-mosses, up to 45 m (150 ft) tall, once formed a large part of the Earth's vegetation (see right). Over 300 million years, their buried remains have gradually turned into coal.

Horsetail

CONTEMPORARY COUSINS
Ferns and horsetails are primitive plants. They do not have flowers, but reproduce by spores. Both first appeared nearly 300 million years ago. Although there are still many types of fern, only about 30 species of horsetail live on Earth today.

Hart's-tongue fern

Spores

Microscopic
view of
duckweed

THE BIGGEST AND THE SMALLEST
The world's most massive plants are conifers –
the giant sequoias of California, which
can reach heights of more than 95 m
(310 ft). The smallest flowering plant
is the rootless duckweed, which is
0.3 mm (¹⁄₁₀₀ in) across.

*Ribbon-like plant body,
or thallus, divides into
branches as it grows*

Garden pansy

LIVERWORTS
Liverworts are non-flowering
plants that live in damp
places and reproduce by
means of spores.

MOSSES
Mosses do not
have flowers. Like
liverworts, mosses
reproduce by
means of
tiny spores.

LIVING SCULPTURES
Algae are simple, non-
flowering plants. A diatom
is a single-celled alga which
has a rigid transparent case,
or frustule, made of silica, a
glass-like substance. This
microscope image shows
many species of diatom, each
of which has a frustule of a
different shape and pattern.

**FLOWERING
PLANTS**
Unlike the other
plants on these two
pages, flowering
plants have true
flowers. They are
also unique in
having seeds that
develop inside a
protective structure
called an ovary (p.17),
which later becomes
a fruit (pp.26–27).
The garden pansy
is a typical
flowering plant.

GREEN BLANKETS
Some species of aquatic
algae form long
chains of cells,
creating a
slime known
as blanket-
weed.

Blanketweed

7

The parts of a plant

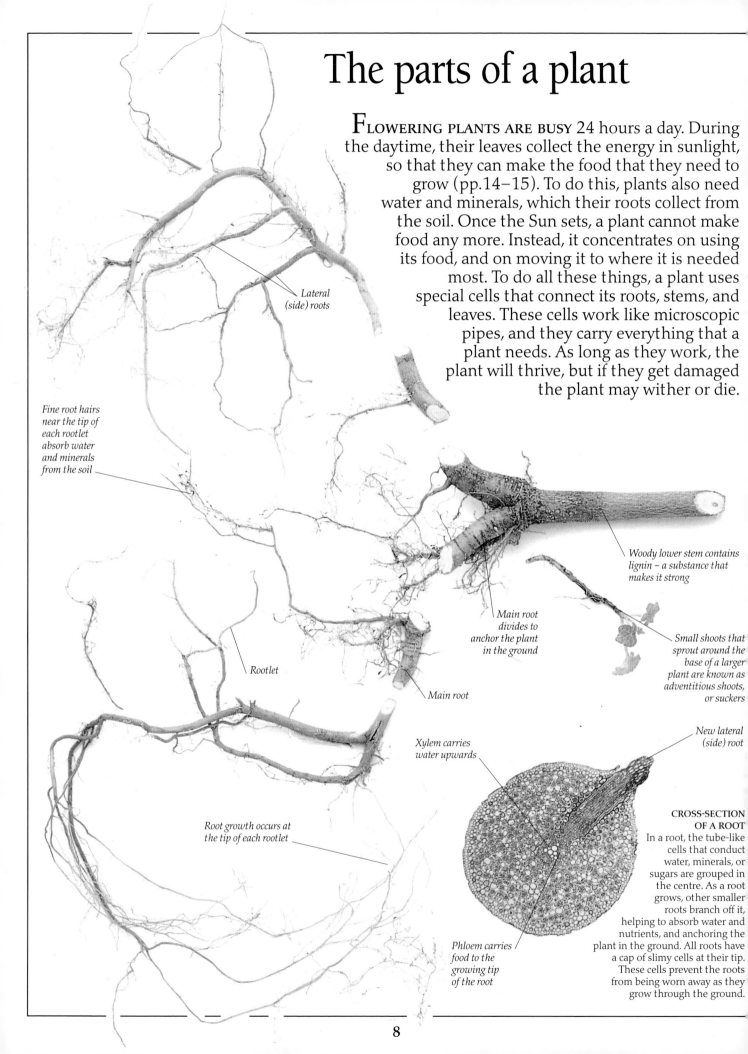

Flowering plants are busy 24 hours a day. During the daytime, their leaves collect the energy in sunlight, so that they can make the food that they need to grow (pp.14–15). To do this, plants also need water and minerals, which their roots collect from the soil. Once the Sun sets, a plant cannot make food any more. Instead, it concentrates on using its food, and on moving it to where it is needed most. To do all these things, a plant uses special cells that connect its roots, stems, and leaves. These cells work like microscopic pipes, and they carry everything that a plant needs. As long as they work, the plant will thrive, but if they get damaged the plant may wither or die.

Lateral (side) roots

Fine root hairs near the tip of each rootlet absorb water and minerals from the soil

Woody lower stem contains lignin – a substance that makes it strong

Main root divides to anchor the plant in the ground

Small shoots that sprout around the base of a larger plant are known as adventitious shoots, or suckers

Rootlet

Main root

Xylem carries water upwards

New lateral (side) root

Root growth occurs at the tip of each rootlet

CROSS-SECTION OF A ROOT
In a root, the tube-like cells that conduct water, minerals, or sugars are grouped in the centre. As a root grows, other smaller roots branch off it, helping to absorb water and nutrients, and anchoring the plant in the ground. All roots have a cap of slimy cells at their tip. These cells prevent the roots from being worn away as they grow through the ground.

Phloem carries food to the growing tip of the root

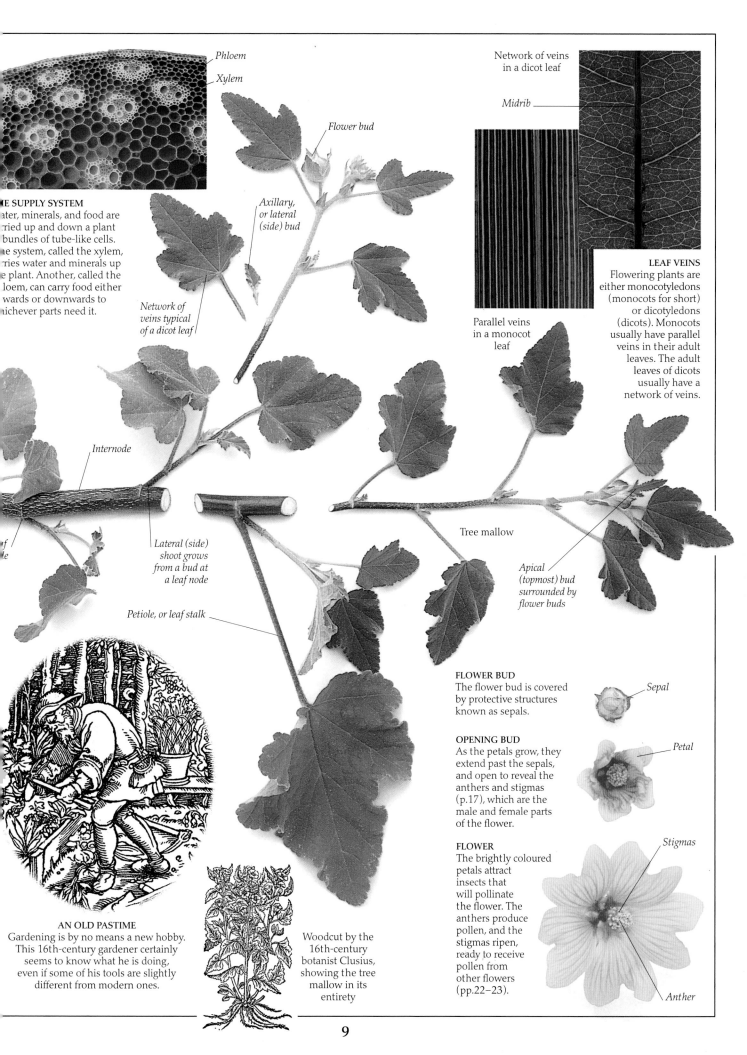

Phloem

Xylem

[TH]E SUPPLY SYSTEM
[W]ater, minerals, and food are
[ca]rried up and down a plant
[in] bundles of tube-like cells.
[On]e system, called the xylem,
[car]ries water and minerals up
[th]e plant. Another, called the
[ph]loem, can carry food either
[up]wards or downwards to
[wh]ichever parts need it.

Flower bud

*Axillary,
or lateral
(side) bud*

*Network of
veins typical
of a dicot leaf*

Network of veins
in a dicot leaf

Midrib

Parallel veins
in a monocot
leaf

LEAF VEINS
Flowering plants are
either monocotyledons
(monocots for short)
or dicotyledons
(dicots). Monocots
usually have parallel
veins in their adult
leaves. The adult
leaves of dicots
usually have a
network of veins.

Internode

Tree mallow

*Lateral (side)
shoot grows
from a bud at
a leaf node*

*Apical
(topmost) bud
surrounded by
flower buds*

Petiole, or leaf stalk

FLOWER BUD
The flower bud is covered
by protective structures
known as sepals.

Sepal

OPENING BUD
As the petals grow, they
extend past the sepals,
and open to reveal the
anthers and stigmas
(p.17), which are the
male and female parts
of the flower.

Petal

FLOWER
The brightly coloured
petals attract
insects that
will pollinate
the flower. The
anthers produce
pollen, and the
stigmas ripen,
ready to receive
pollen from
other flowers
(pp.22–23).

Stigmas

Anther

AN OLD PASTIME
Gardening is by no means a new hobby.
This 16th-century gardener certainly
seems to know what he is doing,
even if some of his tools are slightly
different from modern ones.

Woodcut by the
16th-century
botanist Clusius,
showing the tree
mallow in its
entirety

9

A plant is born

A SEED IS A TINY LIFE-SUPPORT PACKAGE. It contains a plant embryo – the basic parts from which the seedling will develop – together with a supply of food. The food is needed to keep the embryo alive and fuel the process of germination. It is either packed around the embryo, in an endosperm, or stored in special seed-leaves, known as cotyledons. For weeks, months, or even years, the seed may remain inactive. But then, when the conditions are right, it suddenly comes alive and begins to grow. During germination the seed absorbs water, the cells of the embryo start to divide, and eventually the seed case, or testa, breaks open. Firstly, the beginnings of the root system, or radicle, sprouts and grows downwards, followed rapidly by the shoot, or plumule, which will produce the stem and leaves.

First true leaves open out

Terminal bud surrounded by the next pair of leaves

TINY BUT STRONG
When plants grow, they can exert great pressure. Some seedlings can easily push through the tar on the surface of a new road.

Bent plumule

Seed coat, or testa, containing seed leaves

First true leaves

Plumule straightens towards the light

3 HARNESSING THE SUN
With the opening of the first true leaves, the seedling starts to produce its own food by photosynthesis (pp.14–15). Until this time, its growth is fuelled entirely by the food reserves stored in the seed leaves.

First root, or radicle, grows downwards

Main root grows deeper

1 GETTING GOING
The seed of a runner bean will germinate only if it is dark and damp. First the skin of the seed splits. The beginning of the root system, the radicle, appears and starts to grow downwards. Shortly after this, a shoot appears, initially bent double with its tip buried in the seed leaves. This shoot, or plumule, will produce the stem and leaves.

2 REACHING FOR THE LIGHT
As the plumule grows longer, it breaks above ground. Once it is above the soil, it straightens up towards the light, and the first true leaves appear. In the runner bean, the seed leaves stay buried. This is called hypogeal germination. In plants such as the sunflower, the seed-leaves are lifted above ground, where they turn green and start to produce food for the seedling. This is known as epigeal germination.

Root hairs absorb water and minerals from the soil

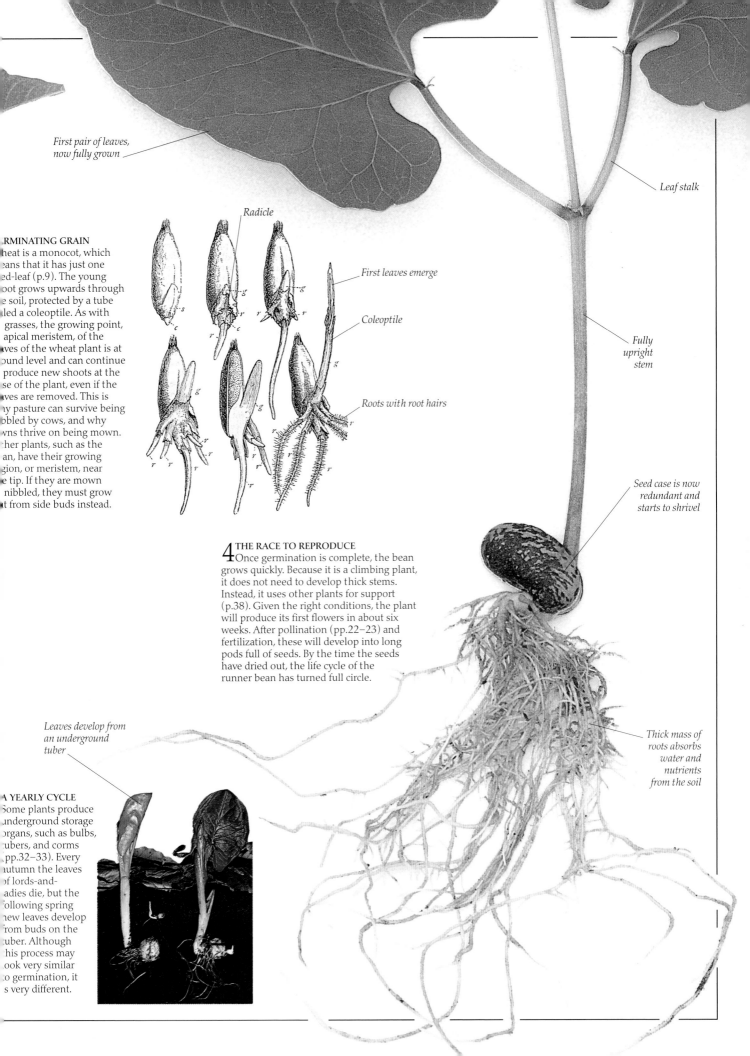

First pair of leaves, now fully grown

Leaf stalk

GERMINATING GRAIN

heat is a monocot, which
eans that it has just one
ed-leaf (p.9). The young
oot grows upwards through
e soil, protected by a tube
led a coleoptile. As with
grasses, the growing point,
apical meristem, of the
ves of the wheat plant is at
ound level and can continue
produce new shoots at the
se of the plant, even if the
ves are removed. This is
y pasture can survive being
bbled by cows, and why
wns thrive on being mown.
her plants, such as the
an, have their growing
gion, or meristem, near
e tip. If they are mown
nibbled, they must grow
t from side buds instead.

Radicle

First leaves emerge

Coleoptile

Roots with root hairs

Fully upright stem

Seed case is now redundant and starts to shrivel

4 THE RACE TO REPRODUCE
Once germination is complete, the bean
grows quickly. Because it is a climbing plant,
it does not need to develop thick stems.
Instead, it uses other plants for support
(p.38). Given the right conditions, the plant
will produce its first flowers in about six
weeks. After pollination (pp.22–23) and
fertilization, these will develop into long
pods full of seeds. By the time the seeds
have dried out, the life cycle of the
runner bean has turned full circle.

Leaves develop from an underground tuber

A YEARLY CYCLE
Some plants produce
underground storage
organs, such as bulbs,
tubers, and corms
(pp.32–33). Every
autumn the leaves
of lords-and-
adies die, but the
ollowing spring
new leaves develop
rom buds on the
tuber. Although
his process may
ook very similar
to germination, it
s very different.

Thick mass of roots absorbs water and nutrients from the soil

Bursting into bloom

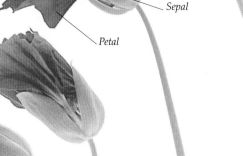

ALL PLANTS HAVE SPECIAL CONTROL SYSTEMS that make sure that they flower at the right time. Some need lots of warmth, and others will only flower after the ground has been soaked by rain. But for many, the most important trigger for flowering is the length of the night. Plants cannot see the difference between night and day, but they can sense it with special chemicals that work like a clock. The length of the night alters with the seasons, so this chemical clock keeps a plant on time. Many plants flower in late spring and early summer, when the days are getting longer, and the nights are getting shorter. At this time of the year, the air is often filled with insects, which makes it an ideal time for flowers to be pollinated. Other plants, such as the garden nasturtium, wait until it is midsummer. This gives them plenty of time to grow before their flowering time arrives. A small number of plants, including chrysanthemums, need short days and long nights before they will flower. They bloom in late summer and early autumn, when most other plants have finished flowering and have already made their seeds.

Petals folded back

New petals unfolding outwards

Sepal

Petal

THE FLOWER OPENS
The garden nasturtium belongs to a family of plants that comes from South America. In countries farther from the equator it flowers in midsummer. When the light conditions are right for the plant, flower buds begin to form. Each flower bud is protected by five sepals. As the bud starts to burst, the sepals open to reveal five bright orange petals that grow outwards and fold back. One of the sepals develops a long spur that lies at the back of the flower. This spur produces nectar, which attracts insect pollinators to the flower.

BLOOMING LOVELY
Markings called honeyguides show insects the way to the nectar. To reach it, the insects have to clamber over the anthers (p.17), which dust them with pollen. As the days pass, the anthers wither and the three stigmas (p.17) become receptive to the pollen of other plants. Insects in search of nectar now dust the stigmas with pollen.

The life cycles of plants

Flowering plants have very different lifespans, ranging from months to centuries. A common poppy will germinate, flower, set seed, and die, all within a single year. Plants that live in this way are known as annuals. Other plants, such as the wild carrot (p.55), take two years to complete the same process. They flower only in their second year – the first is spent growing and building up food reserves, which they store in a thick, fleshy root. These plants are known as biennials. Perennial plants are those that live for a number of years. They include species such as the dandelion (pp.30–31). Perennial weeds are a particular problem for gardeners because their long lifespan gives them time to grow very wide-spreading roots.

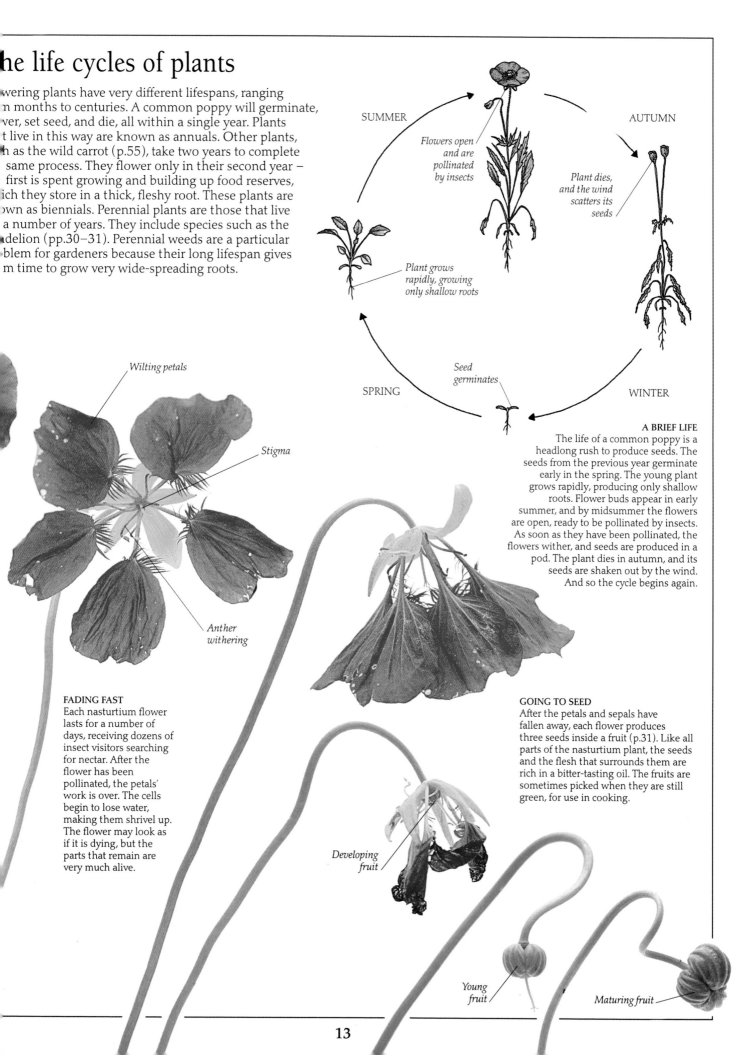

SUMMER

Flowers open and are pollinated by insects

AUTUMN

Plant dies, and the wind scatters its seeds

Plant grows rapidly, growing only shallow roots

Seed germinates

SPRING

WINTER

Wilting petals

Stigma

Anther withering

A BRIEF LIFE
The life of a common poppy is a headlong rush to produce seeds. The seeds from the previous year germinate early in the spring. The young plant grows rapidly, producing only shallow roots. Flower buds appear in early summer, and by midsummer the flowers are open, ready to be pollinated by insects. As soon as they have been pollinated, the flowers wither, and seeds are produced in a pod. The plant dies in autumn, and its seeds are shaken out by the wind. And so the cycle begins again.

FADING FAST
Each nasturtium flower lasts for a number of days, receiving dozens of insect visitors searching for nectar. After the flower has been pollinated, the petals' work is over. The cells begin to lose water, making them shrivel up. The flower may look as if it is dying, but the parts that remain are very much alive.

GOING TO SEED
After the petals and sepals have fallen away, each flower produces three seeds inside a fruit (p.31). Like all parts of the nasturtium plant, the seeds and the flesh that surrounds them are rich in a bitter-tasting oil. The fruits are sometimes picked when they are still green, for use in cooking.

Developing fruit

Young fruit

Maturing fruit

A light diet

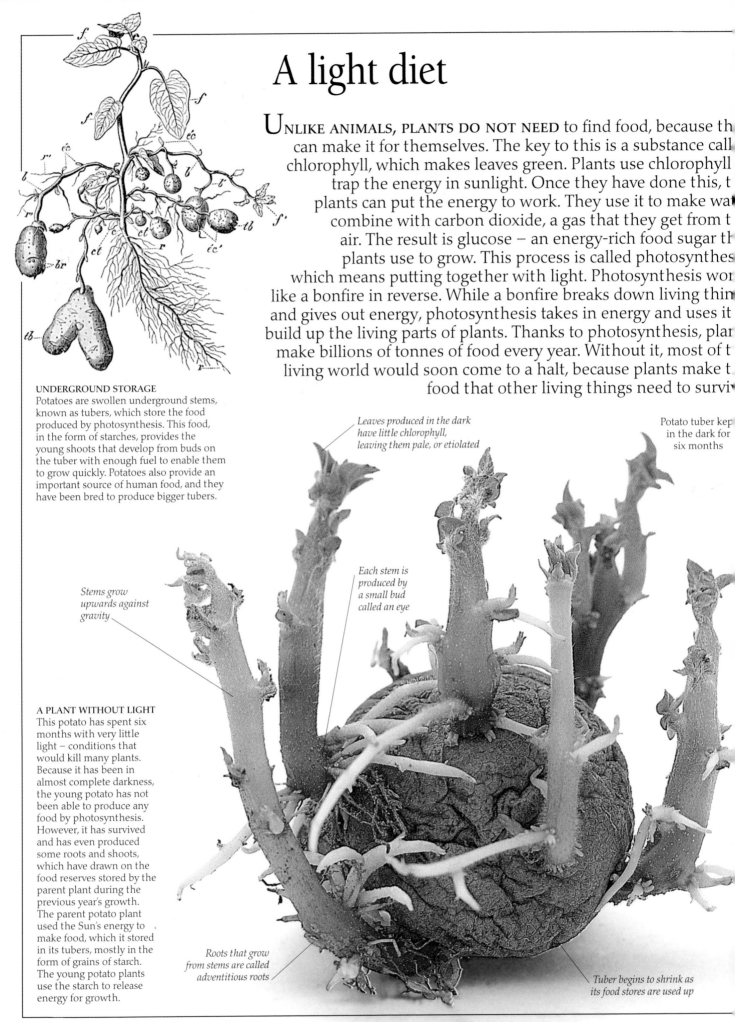

Unlike animals, plants do not need to find food, because th can make it for themselves. The key to this is a substance call chlorophyll, which makes leaves green. Plants use chlorophyll trap the energy in sunlight. Once they have done this, t plants can put the energy to work. They use it to make wat combine with carbon dioxide, a gas that they get from t air. The result is glucose – an energy-rich food sugar th plants use to grow. This process is called photosynthes which means putting together with light. Photosynthesis wor like a bonfire in reverse. While a bonfire breaks down living thin and gives out energy, photosynthesis takes in energy and uses it build up the living parts of plants. Thanks to photosynthesis, plan make billions of tonnes of food every year. Without it, most of t living world would soon come to a halt, because plants make t food that other living things need to survi

UNDERGROUND STORAGE
Potatoes are swollen underground stems, known as tubers, which store the food produced by photosynthesis. This food, in the form of starches, provides the young shoots that develop from buds on the tuber with enough fuel to enable them to grow quickly. Potatoes also provide an important source of human food, and they have been bred to produce bigger tubers.

Leaves produced in the dark have little chlorophyll, leaving them pale, or etiolated

Potato tuber kep in the dark for six months

Each stem is produced by a small bud called an eye

Stems grow upwards against gravity

A PLANT WITHOUT LIGHT
This potato has spent six months with very little light – conditions that would kill many plants. Because it has been in almost complete darkness, the young potato has not been able to produce any food by photosynthesis. However, it has survived and has even produced some roots and shoots, which have drawn on the food reserves stored by the parent plant during the previous year's growth. The parent potato plant used the Sun's energy to make food, which it stored in its tubers, mostly in the form of grains of starch. The young potato plants use the starch to release energy for growth.

Roots that grow from stems are called adventitious roots

Tuber begins to shrink as its food stores are used up

Chloroplasts in cells collect sunlight

Green leaves rich in chlorophyll

PLANT'S SOLAR PANELS
Inside the cells that make up a plant's leaves are tiny structures called chloroplasts. In a single cell, there may be up to a hundred of them. It is inside the chloroplasts that the green, light-trapping pigment chlorophyll is to be found. The chloroplasts work like minute solar panels, collecting the Sun's energy and using it to make food.

STORING SUGAR
Plants store food in various ways – as starches, sugars, or oils. In its first year, an onion plant stores sugars in the onion bulb, which is made up of swollen leaf bases around a shortened stem. In the second year, the sugars in the onion bulb are used up as the plant grows and flowers. The sugars turn brown, or caramelize, when they are heated strongly, which is why onions darken when they are fried.

RAPID REVIVAL
Three weeks after emerging from the dark, the potato plant is now growing rapidly, and its leaves have turned green. This has happened because more chlorophyll has been made in the leaves to harness the energy of the sunlight falling on them. The growing potato plant is now able to collect enough light to build up its own reserves and it no longer needs the energy stored in the old tuber. If the potato were planted now, the energy gathered by its leaves would be stored in the new potato tubers that it would produce, and the old tuber would shrivel and die.

Stems rapidly grow upwards and turn towards the light

Thickening root system

Inside a simple flower

FLOWERS HAVE BECOME extraordinarily varied during the course of evolution. Nature has produced them in a tremendous wealth of shapes and colours. Added to this profusion, people have bred flowers that are even more brilliant or bizarre than the ones found in the wild. But behind this baffling array of shapes and sizes there is a common pattern. For seed production, all flowers use the same underlying structures. The lily flower shown on these two pages is quite simple – its parts are all separate, and they can all be seen clearly. They fall into three groups. The male parts (the stamens) produce the pollen, while the female parts (the carpel) include the ovary, where seeds are produced. Around both the male and the female parts are sepals and petals, which attract insects to the flower.

SIMPLE WHORL
The simplest flowers have their parts arranged in a circle, or whorl.

Stamen

Carpel

Petal from the inner whorl

Open lily flower

Sepal from the outer whorl

When the sepals and petals look the same, they are known as perianth segments, or tepals

THE LILY FAMILY
The lilies and their relatives make up one of the largest families of flowering plants.

Lily flower bud

Stamens and the carpel are packed tightly together

Tepals protecting the male and female parts of the flower

HOW A FLOWER BUD OPENS
In the lily's flower bud, the male and female parts are packed tightly together inside the protective casing formed by the sepals and petals (tepals). The flower bud opens because certain parts of it start to grow more quickly than others. The inside of the base of each tepal, for example, grows faster than the outside. This forces the tepal to bend outwards at the point where it is connected to the flower stalk. At the same time, unequal growth along the edges of each tepal makes the folds in it open out.

Anther produces pollen

Filament

Stamens (male parts)

Stigma receives pollen

Style

Carpel (female parts)

Ovary

Stamens

REPRODUCTIVE PARTS

The lily flower contains both male and female parts. The female parts, or carpels, are at the centre of the flower. They consist of the ovary, where the seeds are produced, and the stigma, which is attached to the ovary by the style. The stigma is the part of the flower that receives pollen during pollination (pp.22–23). The male parts of the flower consist of six identical stamens. Each stamen is made up of an anther, which produces the pollen, supported by a filament. As soon as the pollen is ripe, the anthers split open. When an insect visits the flower, some of the pollen brushes off on to its body and will be carried off to pollinate the stigma of another flower.

Ripe stigma

TAKING TURNS

The male and female parts of a flower often mature at different times. This ensures that the flower does not pollinate itself. Here, the flowers of the wood cranesbill can be seen at three different stages. In the first two stages, the stigma is not ripe, so it cannot be pollinated by the ripe stamens as they bend upright and release their pollen. By the time the stigma is ripe and ready to receive pollen, the stamens have fallen back, having shed all their pollen.

Spotted markings attract pollinating insects

AR ATTRACTION

urrounding the male and male parts of the lily wer is an outer ring, or horl, of three white sepals, d an inner whorl of three hite petals. Because both pals and petals are identical, ey are known as tepals. In e lily flower these tepals ork like advertising signs to tract insects in search of nectar. owever, not all flowers are e this. In many flowers, only e inner whorl of petals is nspicuous. The sepals that make the outer whorl may be tough d green, and protect the flower d. In some plants, the sepals are uch bigger and more colourful an the petals and carry out the sk of attracting insects.

Perianth segments, or tepals, of a lily flower

A complex flower

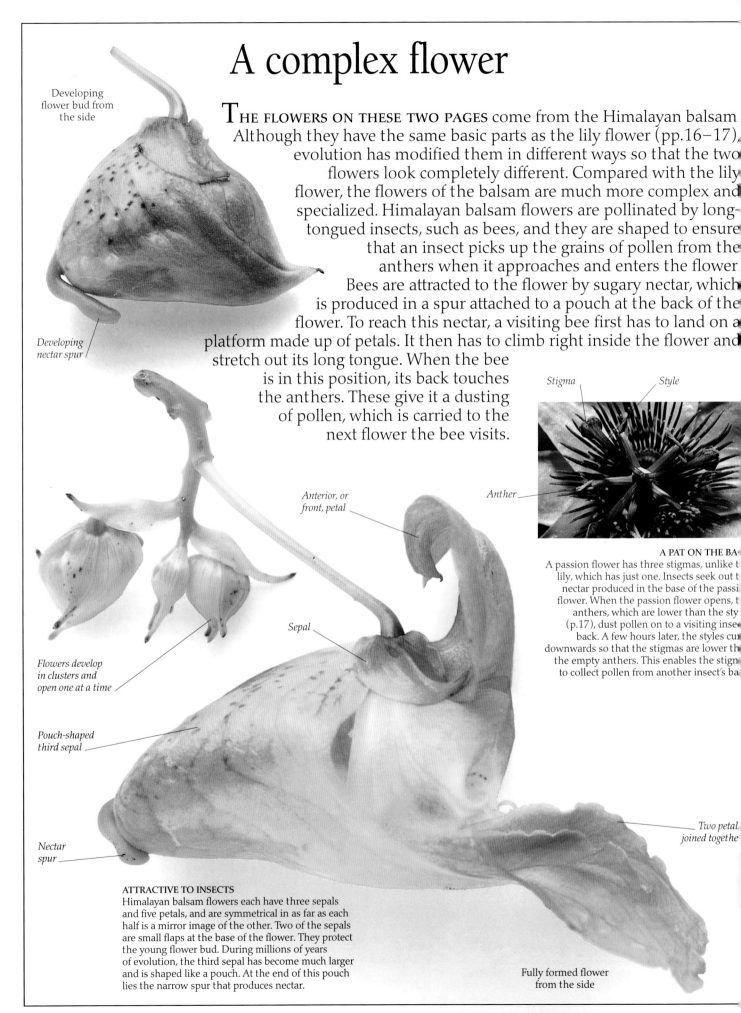

THE FLOWERS ON THESE TWO PAGES come from the Himalayan balsam. Although they have the same basic parts as the lily flower (pp.16–17), evolution has modified them in different ways so that the two flowers look completely different. Compared with the lily flower, the flowers of the balsam are much more complex and specialized. Himalayan balsam flowers are pollinated by long-tongued insects, such as bees, and they are shaped to ensure that an insect picks up the grains of pollen from the anthers when it approaches and enters the flower. Bees are attracted to the flower by sugary nectar, which is produced in a spur attached to a pouch at the back of the flower. To reach this nectar, a visiting bee first has to land on a platform made up of petals. It then has to climb right inside the flower and stretch out its long tongue. When the bee is in this position, its back touches the anthers. These give it a dusting of pollen, which is carried to the next flower the bee visits.

Developing flower bud from the side

Developing nectar spur

Flowers develop in clusters and open one at a time

Pouch-shaped third sepal

Nectar spur

Anterior, or front, petal

Sepal

Stigma

Style

Anther

Two petals joined together

A PAT ON THE BA...
A passion flower has three stigmas, unlike t... lily, which has just one. Insects seek out t... nectar produced in the base of the passi... flower. When the passion flower opens, t... anthers, which are lower than the sty... (p.17), dust pollen on to a visiting inse... back. A few hours later, the styles cu... downwards so that the stigmas are lower th... the empty anthers. This enables the stign... to collect pollen from another insect's ba...

ATTRACTIVE TO INSECTS
Himalayan balsam flowers each have three sepals and five petals, and are symmetrical in as far as each half is a mirror image of the other. Two of the sepals are small flaps at the base of the flower. They protect the young flower bud. During millions of years of evolution, the third sepal has become much larger and is shaped like a pouch. At the end of this pouch lies the narrow spur that produces nectar.

Fully formed flower from the side

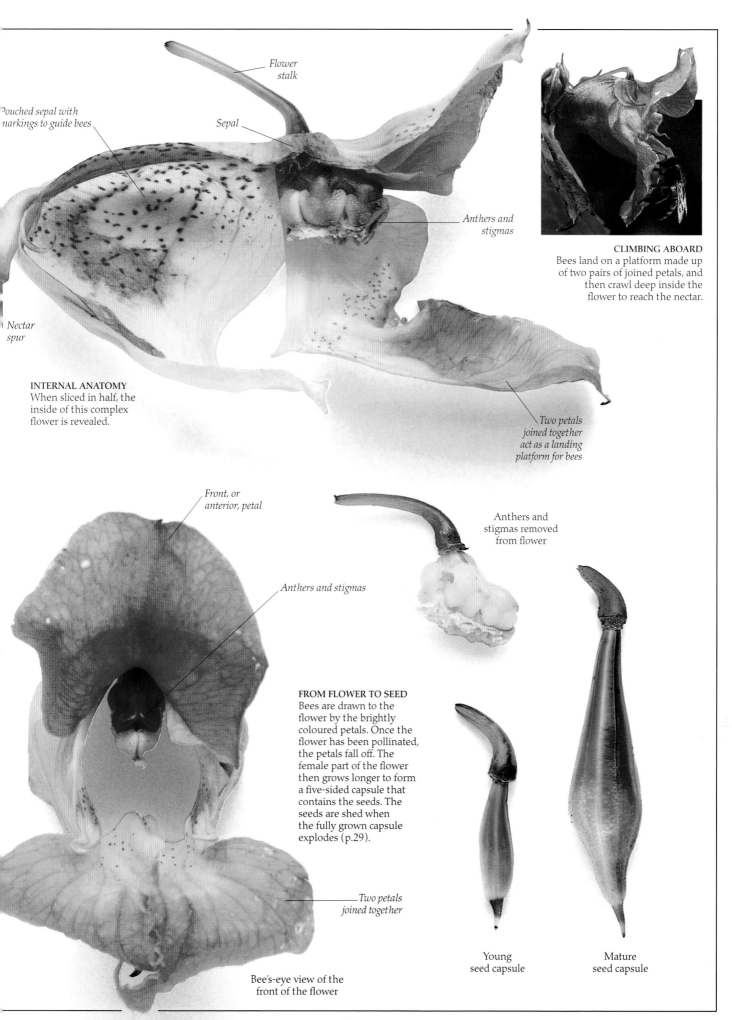

Flower stalk

Pouched sepal with markings to guide bees

Sepal

Anthers and stigmas

CLIMBING ABOARD
Bees land on a platform made up of two pairs of joined petals, and then crawl deep inside the flower to reach the nectar.

Nectar spur

INTERNAL ANATOMY
When sliced in half, the inside of this complex flower is revealed.

Two petals joined together act as a landing platform for bees

Front, or anterior, petal

Anthers and stigmas removed from flower

Anthers and stigmas

FROM FLOWER TO SEED
Bees are drawn to the flower by the brightly coloured petals. Once the flower has been pollinated, the petals fall off. The female part of the flower then grows longer to form a five-sided capsule that contains the seeds. The seeds are shed when the fully grown capsule explodes (p.29).

Two petals joined together

Young seed capsule

Mature seed capsule

Bee's-eye view of the front of the flower

19

All sorts of flowers

Bear's breeches

Petals fused to form tube

HOW MANY INDIVIDUAL FLOWERS are there on these two pages? The question is not quite as simple as it sounds. You would certainly need a magnifying glass to work out the answer, because the final figure adds up to at least 3,300. Some plants, such as the tulip, each have just a single flower. Others, like the dog rose, have a lot of flowers, but each one develops and blooms separately. Many other plants – including most of the plants on these two pages – produce flowers grouped together in clusters known as flower heads. Flower heads have many different shapes, and they vary widely in size and in the number of flowers they contain. The world's biggest individual flower, produced by the giant rafflesia (pp.44–45), is completely dwarfed by the world's biggest flower head this is grown by the rare South American puya which reaches a height of nearly 10 m (33 ft).

Honeysuckle

Mullein

Rosebay willowherb

Dog rose

Individual flower

Individual flower

REGULAR FLOWERS
A regular flower, such as the dog rose (see above), has all its parts – sepals, petals, anthers, and stigma – arranged on a simple circular plan.

Tudor coin

Dog-rose design

The iris is a regular flower that can be cut symmetrically into three pieces

Iris

FLOWER SPIRES
Flowers in spires (see left) usually open in sequence, starting at the bottom. This sequence may take a number of weeks to complete. By the time the last flower has opened, the first may already have set seed.

Sepal

IRREGULAR FLOWERS
An irregular flower, such as the sweet pea, is still symmetrical, but in a more limited way. Most irregular flowers are bilaterally symmetrical, meaning that they can be divided into two halves that are mirror images of each other.

Petal

Sweet pea

lematis

SHOWY TEPALS
The sepals and petals of some flowers, like the clematis, are so similar that it is difficult to tell them apart. These parts are known as tepals (p.16) and may be brightly coloured.

Ray floret with a single ray

White ray florets

Brightly coloured tepal

Disc floret with outer ray florets removed

Disc florets

Eryngo has unusual dome-shaped umbels (flower clusters)

bels
mble
stle
ds

Hogweed has typical umbrella-shaped umbels (flower clusters)

Chamomile, part of the daisy family

COMPOSITE FLOWERS
The flower heads of plants such as sunflowers and daisies are known as composite flowers, because they are composed of many tiny flowers called florets clustered together. Sunflower heads have many hundreds of florets – disc florets in the centre of the flower head, and ray florets, which consist of a single petal-like ray, around the outer edge. In the yarrow (see below), each flower head is made up of many individual disc florets surrounded by about five ray florets. These flower heads are crowded together to form a bigger cluster of about 1,000 florets.

Sunflower

Eryngo

Floret cluster

FLOWERS IN UMBELS
Not only are small flowers more visible when they are clustered together, but flower clusters also provide a better landing platform for pollinating insects. Plants in the family known as the umbellifers, such as hogweed (see right), have their flowers grouped together in umbrella-shaped clusters called umbels. Eryngo (see left) is an unusual umbellifer, since it has dome-shaped umbels.

Hogweed

Cultivated yarrow

How a plant is pollinated

THE FASCINATING SHAPES and brilliant colours of many flowers have evolved over millions of years to make sure that tiny grains of pollen are carried from one plant to another. Pollen grains have to travel from the anthers to the stigma (pp.16–17) for fertilization to occur and for seeds to be produced. Some plants are able to pollinate themselves (self-pollination), but most rely on receiving pollen from another plant of the same species (cross-pollination). Pollen may be dispersed by wind or by water, but the most important pollinators are insects. Plants entice insects to their flowers by their bright colours, and by food in the form of nectar. While the visiting insect feeds, pollen from the anthers is pressed on to its body, often at a particular place such as on the back, or on the head. The stigma of the flower that receives the pollen is in just the right place to collect it as the insect arrives. Some flowers are pollinated by a wide range of insects such as honeybees, bumblebees, hoverflies, and butterflies. Others are more choosy and rely so heavily on a particular pollinator that no other insect species can do the job for them. Some species of yucca, for example, are pollinated exclusively by a small moth, called the yucca moth. In return, the yucca provides the moth with food and a home.

FAMILY HOME
Worker bees bring nectar and pollen back to the hive to feed the developing young

Pollen basket on bee's hind leg

Honeyguide

THE FLORAL FEEDING STATION
Honeyguides (p.12) on the flower guide the bee to the nectar. As the bees feed on the nectar, they also collect pollen in special baskets on their legs so that it can be carried back to the hive.

Bright yellow guide marks show bees where to land

Lower petal acts as a landing platform

OPENING UP
The flower of the common toadflax is pollinated by bumblebees. When a visiting bee arrives, the throat of the flower is tightly closed. To reach the nectar at the back of the flower, the bee must open up the flower by pushing forward.

Nectar tube

CLIMBING IN
As the bumblebee climbs over the hump that seals the flower's throat and crawls inside in search of the nectar, it brushes against the anthers inside the top of the flower. These dust its back with pollen.

FEEDING TIME
As the bee feeds on the flower's nectar, any pollen it is already carrying is transferred from its back to the stigma, and the flower is pollinated.

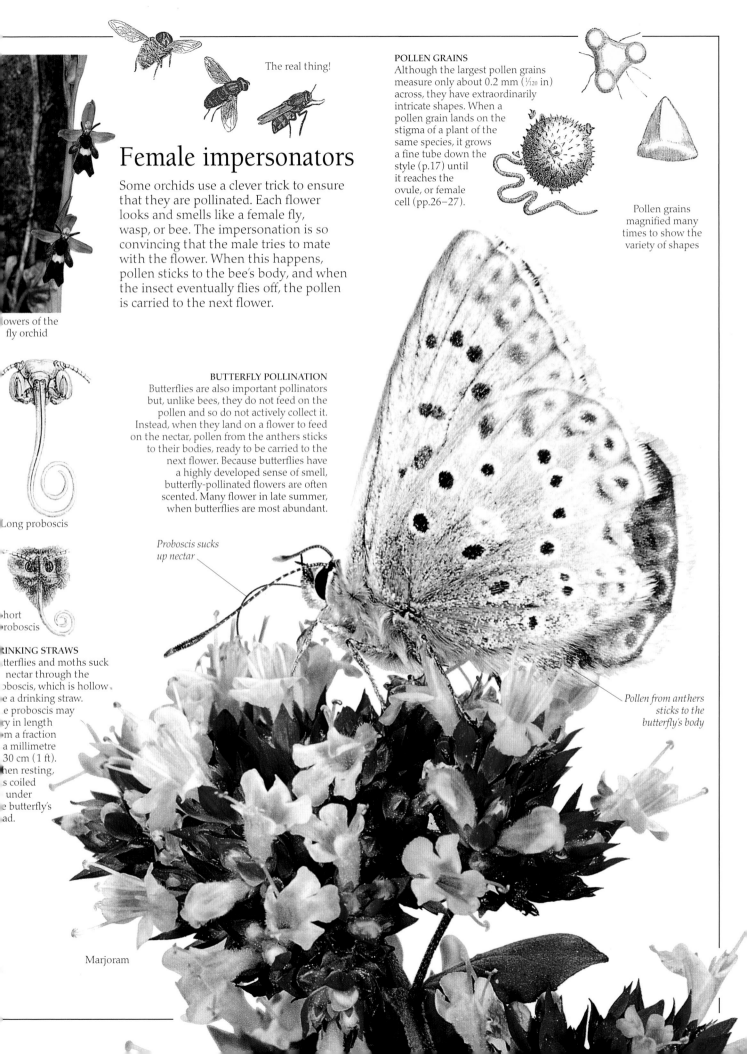

The real thing!

Female impersonators

Some orchids use a clever trick to ensure that they are pollinated. Each flower looks and smells like a female fly, wasp, or bee. The impersonation is so convincing that the male tries to mate with the flower. When this happens, pollen sticks to the bee's body, and when the insect eventually flies off, the pollen is carried to the next flower.

POLLEN GRAINS
Although the largest pollen grains measure only about 0.2 mm (¹⁄₁₂₀ in) across, they have extraordinarily intricate shapes. When a pollen grain lands on the stigma of a plant of the same species, it grows a fine tube down the style (p.17) until it reaches the ovule, or female cell (pp.26–27).

Pollen grains magnified many times to show the variety of shapes

lowers of the
fly orchid

Long proboscis

hort
roboscis

RINKING STRAWS
tterflies and moths suck
nectar through the
oboscis, which is hollow
e a drinking straw.
e proboscis may
ry in length
m a fraction
a millimetre
30 cm (1 ft).
hen resting,
s coiled
under
e butterfly's
ad.

BUTTERFLY POLLINATION
Butterflies are also important pollinators but, unlike bees, they do not feed on the pollen and so do not actively collect it. Instead, when they land on a flower to feed on the nectar, pollen from the anthers sticks to their bodies, ready to be carried to the next flower. Because butterflies have a highly developed sense of smell, butterfly-pollinated flowers are often scented. Many flower in late summer, when butterflies are most abundant.

Proboscis sucks up nectar

Pollen from anthers sticks to the butterfly's body

Marjoram

Strange pollinators

Many flowers are pollinated by bees and butterflies (p.22), but some plant species depend on quite different creatures for pollination. Some are pollinated by the sort of flies that are attracted by the smell of decay. Others rely on birds, which are attracted to the flowers by bright colours and the sweet smell of nectar. Many plants are highly adapted for specific pollinators. The list of these species includes not only insects and birds, but also bats, mice, possums, and even slugs.

DISAPPEARING TRICK

One rare orchid, from Western Australia, spends almost all of its life under ground. It has no leave and its flowers grow in cup-shap clusters that open just level with the surface. The flowers attract termites, gnats, and other insects that help to spread their pollen. After producing their seeds, the flowers wither away, and the orchid disappears below ground once again.

Hairs on the petals attract insects

Flowers are lilac at first, but turn red as they open

Pink bracts attract birds

Shiny surface attracts flies

Cultivated fly-pollinated orchid

Flowers appear among the bracts

A LURE FOR FLIES

Bees are attracted to flowers that have a sweet smell. Many flies, on the other hand, are attracted by the smell of decaying flesh. For this reason, many flowers that rely on flies for pollination have a putrid odour. Some flowers, such as this orchid, have hairs on the surface of their petals to give them an animal-like feel. The shiny surface also attracts flies.

Urn plant

THE RED SIGNAL

Plants that are pollinated by birds often have red or pink petals or flower heads. Birds have excellent colour vision, and a bright red flower, which also produces nectar, readily attracts them. Because this urn plant is one of many plant species that lives high up on trees (p.46), it needs to be conspicuous to attract the attention of the bird pollinators. Most insects, apart from some butterflies, cannot see red, so it is an unusual colour for an insect-pollinated flower.

_Brush-like
anthers_

A BRUSH FOR BIRDS
Most species of hibiscus are pollinated by hummingbirds.
A hummingbird hovers in front of the flower and inserts
its long beak deep inside to reach the nectar. As it feeds,
the anthers brush pollen on to its head, while the stigma,
also brushing its head, collects pollen from another
flower. The flower shown here is in an upright position.
In its natural state it would normally be horizontal.

_Bright yellow spathe
(leaf-like hood) envelops
the flowers on the spadix,
or central spike_

BIZARRE BEAUTY
The yellow calla lily is pollinated by
insects called fungus gnats. Its separate
male and female flowers grow on
a spadix, or central spike, and are
enveloped by a bright yellow leaf-like
hood called a spathe. The insects,
carrying pollen from the male flowers
of other plants, crawl to the base of
the spathe, where they become
trapped by downward-pointing
hairs. As they move around, they
pollinate the female flowers.
The hairs then wither, and
as the insects crawl out
they are dusted with
pollen from the mature
male flowers, ready
to move on to
the next plant.

Hibiscus flower

Yellow
calla lily

POSSUM POLLINATION
The Australian honey possum
is a tiny marsupial that lives
entirely on the pollen and nectar
of flowers like this banksia. It
collects its unusual food with its
long snout and brush-like tongue.
Apart from the possum, the only
other mammals to pollinate
flowers are rodents and bats.

_Translucent,
window-like
cells let
in light_

_Flies fall down this hollow
tube and are trapped by
downward-pointing hairs_

_Trapped flies try
to escape by flying
up towards the
light and become
covered with pollen_

_Landing
flap_

TAKING PRISONERS
This weirdly shaped flower is
produced by a South American
creeper. It lures flies by its smell
of rotting fish. The flies enter the
flower and are imprisoned within
it overnight. When the flower
begins to wither, the flies – now
covered in pollen – can escape.

Brazilian
birthwort

_Colourful lobe (rounded
projection) attracts flies_

Making seeds

PLANTS GROW FLOWERS for an all-important task: to mak
seeds and spread them to new places. Some flowers mak
just one seed, while others can make millions. But n
matter how many they make, the steps they follow ar
usually the same. For most flowers, the first step
pollination (pp.22–23). This transfers tiny mal
pollen grains from flower to flower. If a polle
grain lands on the right kind of flower, ste
two can begin. The pollen grain comes t
life, and grows a microscopic tube dow
through the female part of the flower. Her
it searches out a female cell, or ovule. Onc
the pollen grain has found an ovule, its mal
cells travel down the tube and into the ovul
to fertilize it. The pollen grain has now dor
its work, and the fertilized ovule starts t
turn into a seed. Meanwhile, step thre
gets under way. The flower – nov
without its petals – begins to tur
into a fruit. A fruit is somethin
that helps the seeds to sprea
Some plants produce soft, juic
fruits that attract animal
looking for a meal. Anima
eat the fruit, and they scatte
the seeds as they feed. Man
more plants produce dry, har
fruits that break open whe
they are ripe. These fruits ar
not designed to be eater
Rather, the seeds insid
are spread by othe
means (pp.28–29

**WINTER
FEAST**
Fruits are an
important source
of winter food for many animals. Here,
a redwing feasts on fallen apples and
may help to spread the apples' seeds.

*Sepals
protect the
developing
bud*

EARLY DAYS
Even before the rose comes
into flower, the beginnings
of the rose hip can be seen
clearly. The top of the stem,
to which the flower parts are
attached, is swollen and globular,
as this bud shows. The flower's
female parts, the ovaries and
ovules, are inside this swollen
area, which is called a receptacle.

*Receptacle
containing
ovaries*

Petals open out

*Green sepals
fold back*

THE ROSE IN BLOOM
As the bud opens, the
flower gives off its sweet
scent, which attracts bees
for pollination (pp.22–23).
Once the flower has been
pollinated and the ovules
fertilized, the receptacle
begins to swell.

*Thorns keep
leaf-eating
animals away*

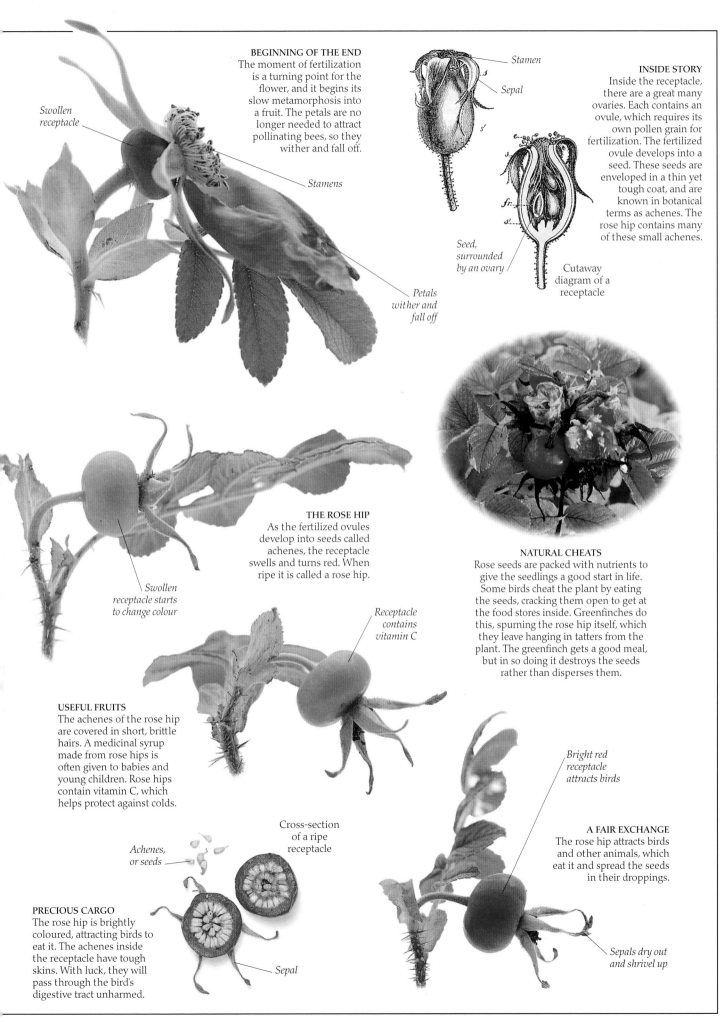

BEGINNING OF THE END
The moment of fertilization is a turning point for the flower, and it begins its slow metamorphosis into a fruit. The petals are no longer needed to attract pollinating bees, so they wither and fall off.

Swollen receptacle

Stamens

Petals wither and fall off

Stamen

Sepal

INSIDE STORY
Inside the receptacle, there are a great many ovaries. Each contains an ovule, which requires its own pollen grain for fertilization. The fertilized ovule develops into a seed. These seeds are enveloped in a thin yet tough coat, and are known in botanical terms as achenes. The rose hip contains many of these small achenes.

Seed, surrounded by an ovary

Cutaway diagram of a receptacle

THE ROSE HIP
As the fertilized ovules develop into seeds called achenes, the receptacle swells and turns red. When ripe it is called a rose hip.

Swollen receptacle starts to change colour

NATURAL CHEATS
Rose seeds are packed with nutrients to give the seedlings a good start in life. Some birds cheat the plant by eating the seeds, cracking them open to get at the food stores inside. Greenfinches do this, spurning the rose hip itself, which they leave hanging in tatters from the plant. The greenfinch gets a good meal, but in so doing it destroys the seeds rather than disperses them.

Receptacle contains vitamin C

USEFUL FRUITS
The achenes of the rose hip are covered in short, brittle hairs. A medicinal syrup made from rose hips is often given to babies and young children. Rose hips contain vitamin C, which helps protect against colds.

Bright red receptacle attracts birds

Cross-section of a ripe receptacle

Achenes, or seeds

A FAIR EXCHANGE
The rose hip attracts birds and other animals, which eat it and spread the seeds in their droppings.

PRECIOUS CARGO
The rose hip is brightly coloured, attracting birds to eat it. The achenes inside the receptacle have tough skins. With luck, they will pass through the bird's digestive tract unharmed.

Sepal

Sepals dry out and shrivel up

How seeds are spread

Agrimony

As ALL GARDENERS KNOW, a patch of bare soil never stays bare for long. Within days, seedlings start to spring up, and if the conditions are right, they eventually cover the ground. Even if the earth is sterilized by heating, so that all the seeds are killed, more somehow arrive and germinate. Plants have evolved some very effective ways of spreading their seeds. In certain plants, exploding seed pods fling the seeds into the air. Others have flying or floating seeds or fruits, which are carried far and wide by the wind and by water currents. Animals also play their part. Many plants have fruits with hooks that stick to fur. The seeds of some species develop inside tasty berries. The berries are eaten by animals and birds, but the seeds pass through the digestive system of these creatures unharmed and fall to the ground, where they germinate.

Lotus seed heads

Seed held in a cup

Dried lotus seed head, seen from above

Fruits have hooks

Each fruit has many tiny hooks

Lesser burdock

Lotuses growing in ancient Egypt

HITCHING A LIFT
The best way to find out which seeds are dispersed by animals is to go for a walk through rough grassland. You will probably return home with the fruits of a number of different plants stuck to your clothes. Known as burrs, these fruits have hooks and spines that cling to the fur and wool of passing animals. When the burrs are rubbed or scratched off, their seeds fall to the ground and germinate.

Burrs clinging to the fur on a dog's back

WASHED AWAY
The lotus is a water plant that produces its seeds in a flattened head. When the seeds are ripe, they fall on to the water's surface and float away. Lotus seeds can be extraordinarily long-lived. Some have been known to germinate more than 200 years after they were shed.

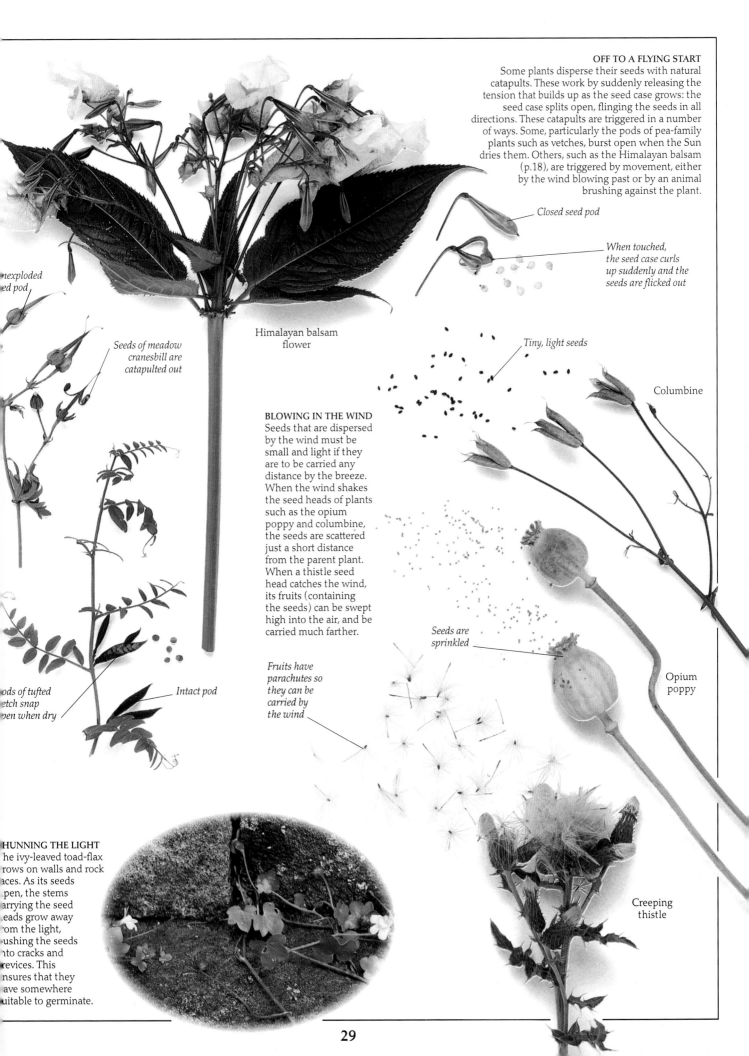

Some plants disperse their seeds with natural catapults. These work by suddenly releasing the tension that builds up as the seed case grows: the seed case splits open, flinging the seeds in all directions. These catapults are triggered in a number of ways. Some, particularly the pods of pea-family plants such as vetches, burst open when the Sun dries them. Others, such as the Himalayan balsam (p.18), are triggered by movement, either by the wind blowing past or by an animal brushing against the plant.

Closed seed pod

When touched, the seed case curls up suddenly and the seeds are flicked out

nexploded ed pod

Himalayan balsam flower

Seeds of meadow cranesbill are catapulted out

Tiny, light seeds

Columbine

BLOWING IN THE WIND
Seeds that are dispersed by the wind must be small and light if they are to be carried any distance by the breeze. When the wind shakes the seed heads of plants such as the opium poppy and columbine, the seeds are scattered just a short distance from the parent plant. When a thistle seed head catches the wind, its fruits (containing the seeds) can be swept high into the air, and be carried much farther.

Seeds are sprinkled

Opium poppy

ods of tufted etch snap en when dry

Intact pod

Fruits have parachutes so they can be carried by the wind

HUNNING THE LIGHT
he ivy-leaved toad-flax rows on walls and rock aces. As its seeds pen, the stems arrying the seed eads grow away rom the light, ushing the seeds nto cracks and revices. This nsures that they ave somewhere uitable to germinate.

Creeping thistle

Borne on the wind

ACCORDING TO TRADITION, if you blow on a dandelion's seed head, the number of puffs needed to blow away all the seeds will tell you the time of day. Whether or not this is true, it is a custom that certainly helps the plant to spread. The seeds of the dandelion are encased in tiny fruits and have their own special feathery parachutes to help them float through the air. If you blow on them, you may be starting the seeds on a journey that takes them high up and far away. The dandelion's flower, like that of the sunflower (p.21), is actually a composite flower head made up of many tiny florets. Each of the florets produces a single fruit. Like the dandelion, many other composite plants, such as hawkweeds, ragworts, and thistles, rely on the wind to disperse their seeds. The fruits of some of these have parachutes; others have fine hairs that stick out in all directions to form a feathery ball. Many of these plants are troublesome weeds because they quickly colonize bare soil in gardens and on farmland.

Dandelion fruits floating away on the breeze

1 OPENING TIME
The dandelion's flower opens in the morning and closes in the afternoon or when it rains. The plant's name comes from the French *dent de lion,* meaning lion's tooth, which describes the jagged edges of the leaves.

Flower closes before the seeds form

Flower head open, waiting to be pollinated by a passing insect

2 THE SEEDS START TO FORM
After opening and closing for a number of days, during which time it may be pollinated, the flower finally closes, and seed formation begins. Gradually the yellow petals wither away, and the pappus, which is the name given to the small circle of hairs attached to the top of each fruit, starts to grow longer. This is the beginning of the parachute.

Bracts protect the developing seed head

30

Seed head opens when the parachutes are formed

Bracts fold back

3 OPENING OUT
The seed head begins to open only when the weather is dry. At first, the parachutes are squashed together, but as the bracts around the edge of the seed head fold back, the parachutes begin to expand.

4 READY TO GO
If the air is still, the fruits may spend several days attached to the seed head. This is a dangerous time for them, because seed-eating birds such as goldfinches are likely to peck them off and eat them.

Fully opened seed head

Parachutes attached to tiny fruits

5 LIFT OFF
A slight breeze is all that is needed to lift the parachutes into the air. They may fall close by, but if there is enough updraught they can be carried for long distances. When a fruit lands, it no longer needs the parachute that has carried it on its journey, and this breaks off. Over the winter the seed sinks into the soil, waiting for the spring when it begins to germinate.

Spreading without seeds

Creeping buttercup

PLANTS CAN REPRODUCE in two quite different ways. As well as reproducing by means of seeds, they can sometimes also turn small pieces of themselves into new plants. This is known as vegetative reproduction. When a plant reproduces in this way, the young plantlets are genetically identical to the parent. This is quite different from reproduction with seeds, which produces seedlings that are all slightly different from their parents. Vegetative reproduction is very useful for farmers and gardeners. It means that they can multiply a plant that has attractive flowers or tasty fruit, knowing that each young plant will have exactly the characteristics they want. The world's oldest plants all grow by forming clumps, another form of vegetative reproduction. In the southwestern United States, there are clumps of creosote bushes up to 12,000 years old, which makes them about twice as old as the oldest single trees. In Tasmania, Australia, some clumps of king's holly are more than 40,000 years old, and still growing strong.

THE PIGGYBACK PLANT
The piggyback plant has an unusual way of reproducing. Tiny new plantlets grow at the base of the older leaves and look as though they are having a piggyback ride.

Parent plant

CREEPING STEMS
Some plants, such as the creeping buttercup, spread by means of stolons, which are leafy stems that grow along the ground. When the stolons reach a certain length, a new, young plant develops from a bud at the leaf node (p.9), and the stolon eventually withers away completely.

Fallen plantlets

Strawberry plant

Parent plant

Stolon, or runner

Bud at a leaf node

Chandelier plant

PLANTLETS AT LEAF TIPS
Kalanchoes are succulents (p.53), many of which reproduce by developing tiny plantlets along the edges of their leaves. Others, like this chandelier plant, have them just at the tips. When a plantlet is mature, it falls off the parent plant and takes root in the soil beneath.

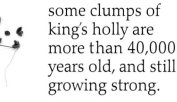

STRAWBERRY RUNNERS
After they have fruited, strawberry plants produce long stolons known as runners, which spread out over the ground. Strawberry growers wait until the young plants have rooted and then cut the runners. The new plants can be transplanted to make a new strawberry bed.

A MYTH EXPLODED
The famous tumbleweed of the North American prairies is uprooted by strong winds after it has flowered and is often blown far away from the place where it grew. The dead plant cannot put down roots once it comes to a halt, as is often supposed. Instead, it spreads by seeds. The plant scatters them as it tumbles along the ground.

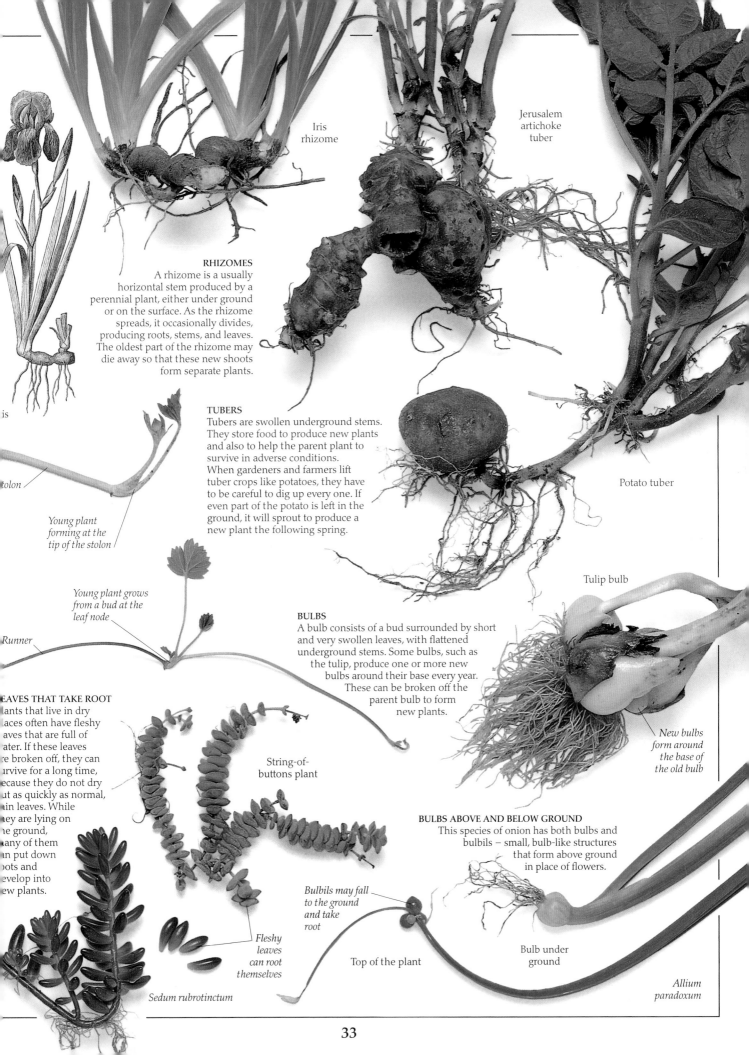

Iris
rhizome

Jerusalem
artichoke
tuber

RHIZOMES
A rhizome is a usually
horizontal stem produced by a
perennial plant, either under ground
or on the surface. As the rhizome
spreads, it occasionally divides,
producing roots, stems, and leaves.
The oldest part of the rhizome may
die away so that these new shoots
form separate plants.

is

tolon

*Young plant
forming at the
tip of the stolon*

TUBERS
Tubers are swollen underground stems.
They store food to produce new plants
and also to help the parent plant to
survive in adverse conditions.
When gardeners and farmers lift
tuber crops like potatoes, they have
to be careful to dig up every one. If
even part of the potato is left in the
ground, it will sprout to produce a
new plant the following spring.

Potato tuber

*Young plant grows
from a bud at the
leaf node*

Runner

Tulip bulb

BULBS
A bulb consists of a bud surrounded by short
and very swollen leaves, with flattened
underground stems. Some bulbs, such as
the tulip, produce one or more new
bulbs around their base every year.
These can be broken off the
parent bulb to form
new plants.

EAVES THAT TAKE ROOT
lants that live in dry
laces often have fleshy
aves that are full of
ater. If these leaves
re broken off, they can
rvive for a long time,
ecause they do not dry
ut as quickly as normal,
in leaves. While
ey are lying on
e ground,
any of them
n put down
ots and
velop into
ew plants.

String-of-
buttons plant

*New bulbs
form around
the base of
the old bulb*

BULBS ABOVE AND BELOW GROUND
This species of onion has both bulbs and
bulbils – small, bulb-like structures
that form above ground
in place of flowers.

*Bulbils may fall
to the ground
and take
root*

*Fleshy
leaves
can root
themselves*

Top of the plant

Bulb under
ground

*Allium
paradoxum*

Sedum rubrotinctum

33

Living leaves

LEAVES ARE SO VARIED that botanists have invented a whole new language to describe their shapes and the way they are fixed to plants. One reason for all this variety is that each species of plant faces its own chalenges in harvesting sunlight (pp.14–15). A plant living on the gloomy floor of a rainforest, for example, may need big leaves to catch enough light. A plant growing on top of a cliff has plenty of light, but it is lashed by strong winds, so it needs small, strong leaves if it is to survive. Some plants have more than one type of leaf. This is most marked in plants that start their lives under water but then flower above it. One example is the water crowfoot. Its submerged leaves are fine and feathery, to let water flow past without tearing them, while its upper leaves are flat and broad, so that they float on the surface.

FEATHERY LEAVES
Water plants often have feathery leaves to allow the water to flow past without damaging them.

CHANGING COLOUR
The leaves of herb Robert change from green to crimson as autumn approaches, or in very dry weather.

PARALLEL VEINS
The leaves of plants such as grasses, orchids, and lilies have parallel veins (p.9). These strap-like leaves are from a member of the lily family.

FURRY LEAVES
Some leaves have a fur-like covering that helps to reduce water loss. These leaves are from a cultivated pyrethrum, which is grown in gardens.

Older leaves

Young leaves

DIFFERE[NT] SHA[PES]
This eucalyp[tus] tree has lea[ves] of two tota[lly] different shap[es]. The leaves of [the] young stems [are] round, like coins, a[nd] each one complet[ely] encircles the bran[ch]. The leaves on [the] older parts of t[he] stems have sta[lks] and are shap[ed] like sh[arp] stra[ps].

Leaf supported by strong ribs

FACING THE WIND
Wild asparagus lives on windy coasts. Instead of true leaves it has feathery, green, leaf-like stems, called cladodes, which can withstand gales. Large, fleshy leaves would be torn to pieces.

WATERSIDE GIANTS
Gunneras grow on river-banks in tropical forests, but are sometimes found beside water in warmer parts of temperate countries. Their leaves can be enormous – as much as 2 m (6 ft) in diameter.

Wild asparagus

Underside of a section of a gunnera leaf

Leaflet

COMPOUND LEAF
Leaves made up of a number of individual leaflets are known as compound leaves.

SLASHED LEAVES
The Swiss cheese plant grows in tropical forests, clinging to trees for support. It probably gets its name from its unusual leaves. With all their slashes and perforations, they are reminiscent of some types of very holey Swiss cheese.

Waxy upper surface

SIMPLE LEAF
Leaves without leaflets are known as simple leaves.

Slashes appear as the leaf grows older

PELTATE LEAF
Circular leaves with the stalk inserted in the middle are said to be peltate.

EVERGREEN LEAVES
Evergreen plants do not lose their leaves in the winter, so their leaves need to be tough to survive several years in the wind, Sun, and rain. Rhododendron leaves have a waxy upper surface to prevent them from drying out, and some species also have felt-like down on their undersides to retain moisture and keep insects away.

Joseph's coat

Lungwort

Some varieties have red undersides

Rhododendron leaves

Downy underside

MULTICOLOURED LEAVES
Variegated, or multicoloured, leaves are often found in garden plants. The lungwort gets its name from its spotty leaves, which give it the appearance of a human lung. In the past, it was also used as a cure for lung diseases.

Self-defence

PLANTS CANNOT RUN AWAY from their enemies in the same way that animals do, so they have evolved special weapons and armour to protect themselves. The main enemies of most plants are the animals that feed on them. These range in size from tiny insects that suck sap, or chew their way through leaves, to large mammals that eat entire plants. To keep the smallest enemies at bay, many plants have a mat of fine hairs on the surface of their leaves. Larger animals are deterred by means of special weaponry, including spines, thorns, and stings. As a final defence, many plants have chemicals in their cells that make them unpleasant to eat. Once an animal has tasted the plant, it is unlikely to want to repeat the experience.

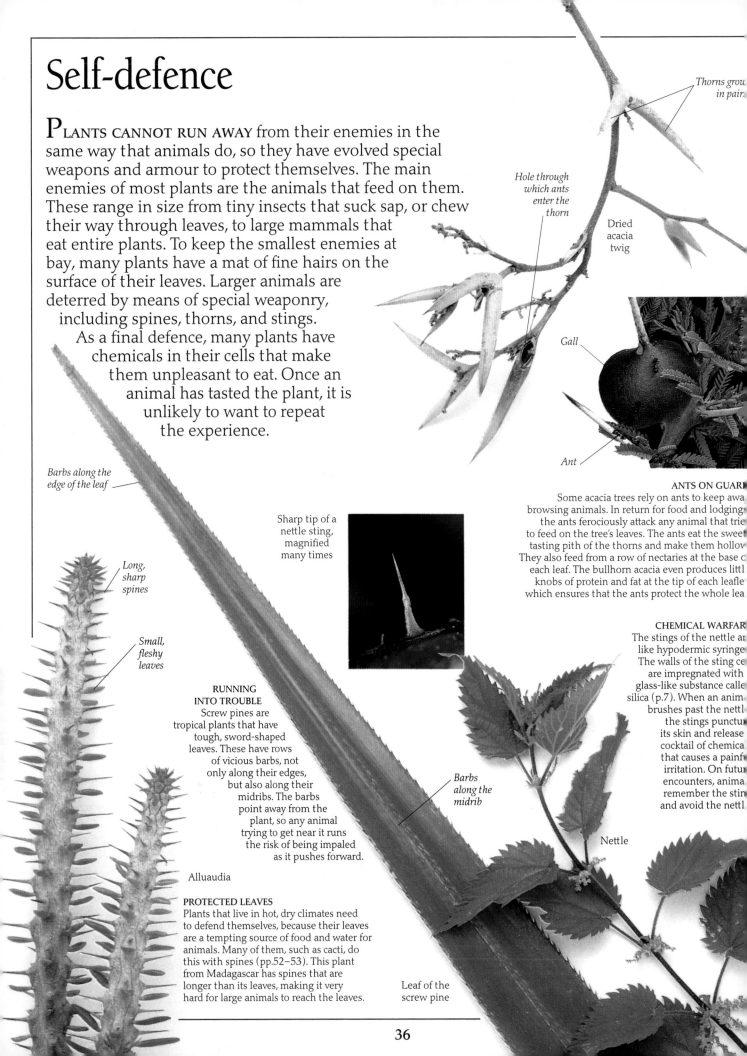

Thorns grow in pair

Hole through which ants enter the thorn

Dried acacia twig

Gall

Ant

Barbs along the edge of the leaf

Long, sharp spines

Small, fleshy leaves

Sharp tip of a nettle sting, magnified many times

RUNNING INTO TROUBLE
Screw pines are tropical plants that have tough, sword-shaped leaves. These have rows of vicious barbs, not only along their edges, but also along their midribs. The barbs point away from the plant, so any animal trying to get near it runs the risk of being impaled as it pushes forward.

Alluaudia

PROTECTED LEAVES
Plants that live in hot, dry climates need to defend themselves, because their leaves are a tempting source of food and water for animals. Many of them, such as cacti, do this with spines (pp.52–53). This plant from Madagascar has spines that are longer than its leaves, making it very hard for large animals to reach the leaves.

Barbs along the midrib

Leaf of the screw pine

ANTS ON GUARD
Some acacia trees rely on ants to keep awa browsing animals. In return for food and lodging the ants ferociously attack any animal that trie to feed on the tree's leaves. The ants eat the swee tasting pith of the thorns and make them hollov They also feed from a row of nectaries at the base each leaf. The bullhorn acacia even produces littl knobs of protein and fat at the tip of each leafle which ensures that the ants protect the whole lea

CHEMICAL WARFAR
The stings of the nettle ar like hypodermic syringe The walls of the sting ce are impregnated with glass-like substance calle silica (p.7). When an anim brushes past the nettl the stings punctu its skin and release cocktail of chemica that causes a painf irritation. On futur encounters, anima remember the stin and avoid the nettl

Nettle

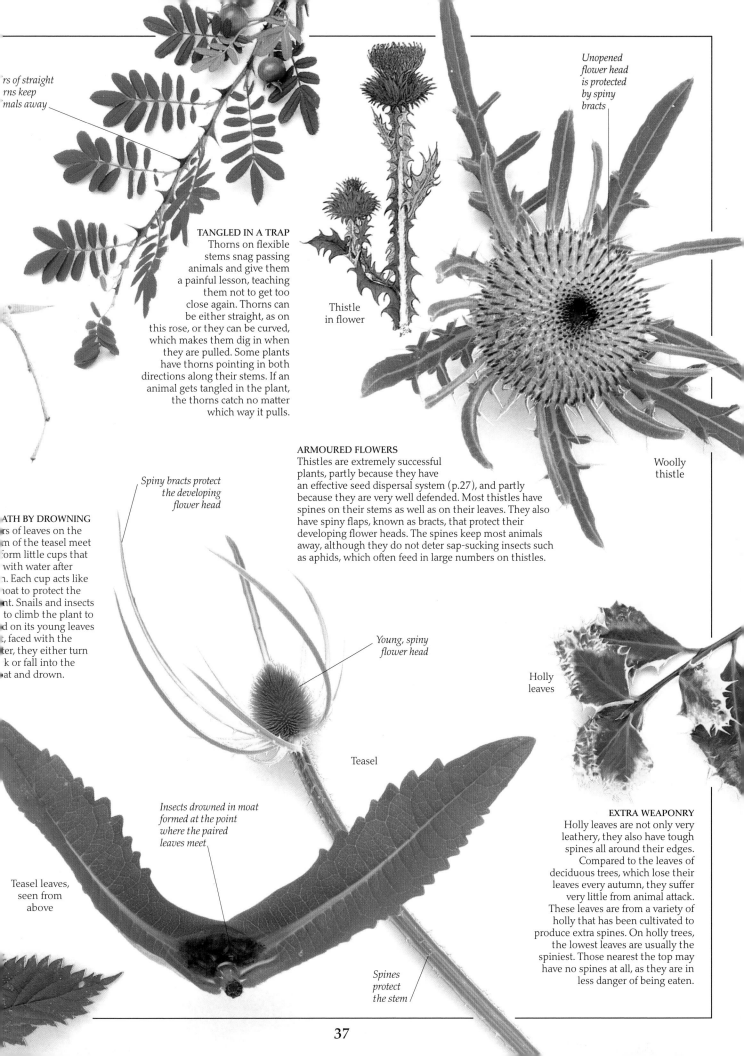

*...rs of straight
...rns keep
...mals away*

TANGLED IN A TRAP
Thorns on flexible
stems snag passing
animals and give them
a painful lesson, teaching
them not to get too
close again. Thorns can
be either straight, as on
this rose, or they can be curved,
which makes them dig in when
they are pulled. Some plants
have thorns pointing in both
directions along their stems. If an
animal gets tangled in the plant,
the thorns catch no matter
which way it pulls.

Thistle
in flower

*Unopened
flower head
is protected
by spiny
bracts*

Woolly
thistle

ARMOURED FLOWERS
Thistles are extremely successful
plants, partly because they have
an effective seed dispersal system (p.27), and partly
because they are very well defended. Most thistles have
spines on their stems as well as on their leaves. They also
have spiny flaps, known as bracts, that protect their
developing flower heads. The spines keep most animals
away, although they do not deter sap-sucking insects such
as aphids, which often feed in large numbers on thistles.

*...ATH BY DROWNING
...rs of leaves on the
...m of the teasel meet
...orm little cups that
...with water after
...n. Each cup acts like
...oat to protect the
...nt. Snails and insects
...to climb the plant to
...d on its young leaves
...t, faced with the
...ter, they either turn
...k or fall into the
...at and drown.*

*Spiny bracts protect
the developing
flower head*

*Young, spiny
flower head*

Holly
leaves

Teasel

Teasel leaves,
seen from
above

*Insects drowned in moat
formed at the point
where the paired
leaves meet*

*Spines
protect
the stem*

EXTRA WEAPONRY
Holly leaves are not only very
leathery, they also have tough
spines all around their edges.
Compared to the leaves of
deciduous trees, which lose their
leaves every autumn, they suffer
very little from animal attack.
These leaves are from a variety of
holly that has been cultivated to
produce extra spines. On holly trees,
the lowest leaves are usually the
spiniest. Those nearest the top may
have no spines at all, as they are in
less danger of being eaten.

Creepers and climbers

Wherever there is moisture and warmth, plants struggle against each other for light. The tallest plant usually gets the greatest share, but it also has to spend the most energy in growing a strong stem, or a tree trunk, to hold up its leaves. But there are some plants – epiphytes (pp.46–47) and climbers – that take a short cut to the top. They take advantage of other plants and even buildings to get a place in the light with much less effort. Epiphytes may grow on the trunks or upper branches of trees and are lifted up with them as they grow. These plants do not have roots on the ground and are able to absorb all the water they need from the air and rainwater. Climbers need supports. Some twine themselves around a plant, while others put out touch-sensitive feelers, or tendrils, that curl around the support when they come into contact with it. A third group of climbers raise themselves by means of stiff side branches, prickles, roots, or hairs.

GROWING IN A SPIRAL
Plants that grow in a spiral will twist in a set direction. Runner bean plant always twist in a clockwise direction a detail noticed by the artist who made this 16th-century woodcut of a bean plant climbing up a stick.

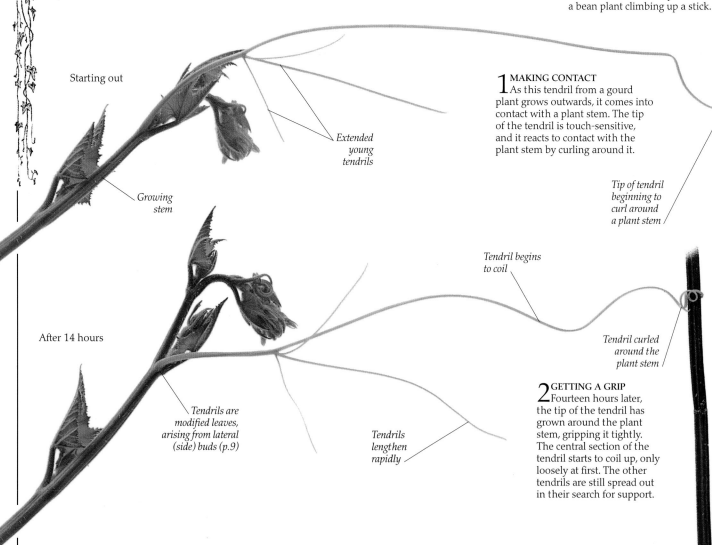

Starting out

Extended young tendrils

Growing stem

After 14 hours

Tendrils are modified leaves, arising from lateral (side) buds (p.9)

Tendrils lengthen rapidly

1 MAKING CONTACT
As this tendril from a gourd plant grows outwards, it comes into contact with a plant stem. The tip of the tendril is touch-sensitive, and it reacts to contact with the plant stem by curling around it.

Tip of tendril beginning to curl around a plant stem

Tendril begins to coil

Tendril curled around the plant stem

2 GETTING A GRIP
Fourteen hours later, the tip of the tendril has grown around the plant stem, gripping it tightly. The central section of the tendril starts to coil up, only loosely at first. The other tendrils are still spread out in their search for support.

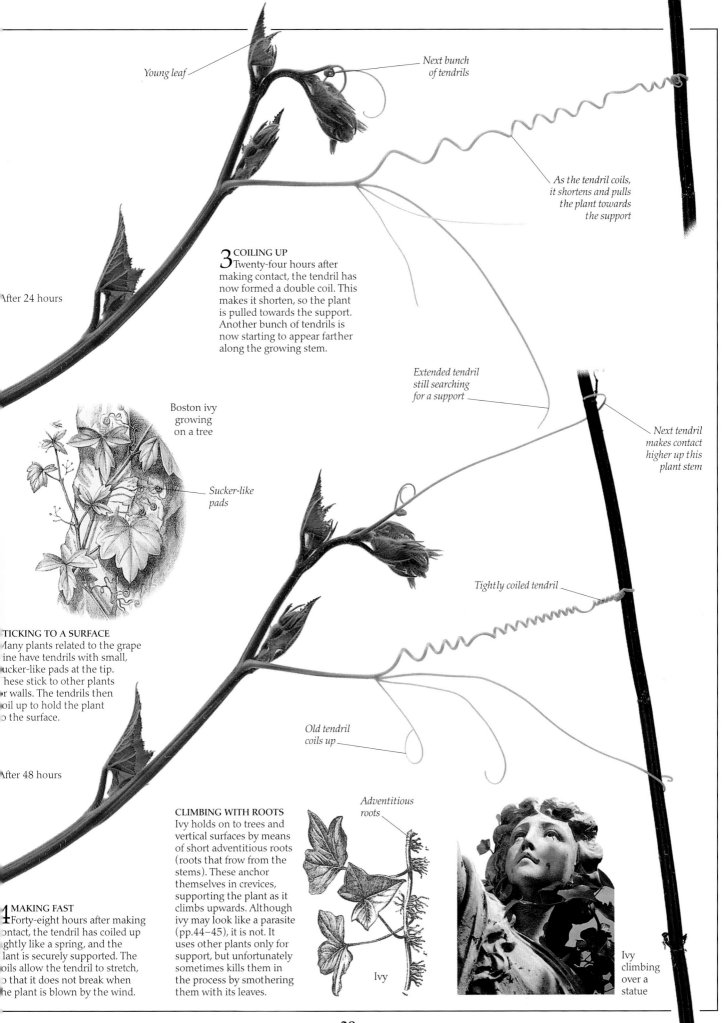

Young leaf

Next bunch of tendrils

As the tendril coils, it shortens and pulls the plant towards the support

After 24 hours

3 COILING UP
Twenty-four hours after making contact, the tendril has now formed a double coil. This makes it shorten, so the plant is pulled towards the support. Another bunch of tendrils is now starting to appear farther along the growing stem.

Extended tendril still searching for a support

Boston ivy growing on a tree

Next tendril makes contact higher up this plant stem

Sucker-like pads

Tightly coiled tendril

ſTICKING TO A SURFACE
Ⅿany plants related to the grape ⅴine have tendrils with small, ſucker-like pads at the tip. Ｔhese stick to other plants ⲟr walls. The tendrils then ⲟil up to hold the plant ⲟ the surface.

After 48 hours

Old tendril coils up

4 MAKING FAST
Forty-eight hours after making ⲟntact, the tendril has coiled up ⲟghtly like a spring, and the ⲟlant is securely supported. The ⲟoils allow the tendril to stretch, ⲟ that it does not break when ⲟhe plant is blown by the wind.

CLIMBING WITH ROOTS
Ivy holds on to trees and vertical surfaces by means of short adventitious roots (roots that frow from the stems). These anchor themselves in crevices, supporting the plant as it climbs upwards. Although ivy may look like a parasite (pp.44–45), it is not. It uses other plants only for support, but unfortunately sometimes kills them in the process by smothering them with its leaves.

Adventitious roots

Ivy

Ivy climbing over a statue

Meat eaters

ALTHOUGH MAN-EATING PLANTS belong to
the world of fiction, there are many plants
that eat insects and other small animals.
These carnivorous, or meat-eating, plants
fall into two groups. Some species, such as
the Venus flytrap (pp.42–43), have active
traps, with moving parts that catch their
prey. Other species have inactive traps with
no moving parts. They simply attract their
victims with a scent reminiscent of food,
and then catch them on a sticky surface or
drown them in a pool of fluid. The victims of
carnivorous plants are mostly insects. Once an
insect has been caught, it is slowly dissolved by
digestive fluids produced by the plant. After many
days, all that is left is the insect's exoskeleton – the
hard outer casing of the body. The rest of the insect
has been absorbed by the plant. Carnivorous plants
can make food from sunlight like ordinary plants.
The insects they catch are simply used as an extra
source of food because they grow in waterlogged
ground, where the soil is deficient in nitrates
and other essential nutrients.

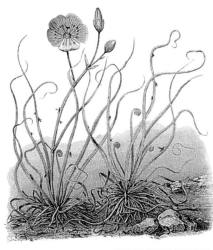

SPECIALIZED LEAVES
All the animal traps shown on
these two pages are modified
leaves. The leaves of the
Portuguese sundew are so sticky
that people used to hang them up
indoors to catch flies.

*Flower of the
Cape sundew*

*Lid kee[ps]
out the
rain*

Rim

FATAL ATTRACTION
This colourful nepenthes
pitcher lures passing insects.

*Water flea
trapped by a
bladderwort*

THE STICKY SUNDEWS
The leaves of sundews are covered
in hairs that produce droplets of
sticky glue. When an insect lands
on one of the leaves, it sticks
to the hairs, which then
fold over, trapping it.

UNDERWATER TRAPS
Bladderworts are water
plants that develop
traps, in the form of
tiny bladders, on their
feathery leaves. If a small
water animal swims past,
the bubble-like bladder
snaps open, and the animal
is sucked inside.

Magnified view
of a fly trapped
by hairs on a
sundew leaf

Cape
sundew

LYING IN WAIT
Butterworts have circles of flat, sticky
leaves. These plants may not look
very threatening, but when an insect
lands on a leaf, it becomes glued
to the surface and eventually
dies. The edges of the leaf very
gradually curl inwards, and
the insect is digested. There
are about 50 species of
butterwort, most of which
grow in marshy places.

*Leaf covered with
short, sticky hairs*

Butterwort

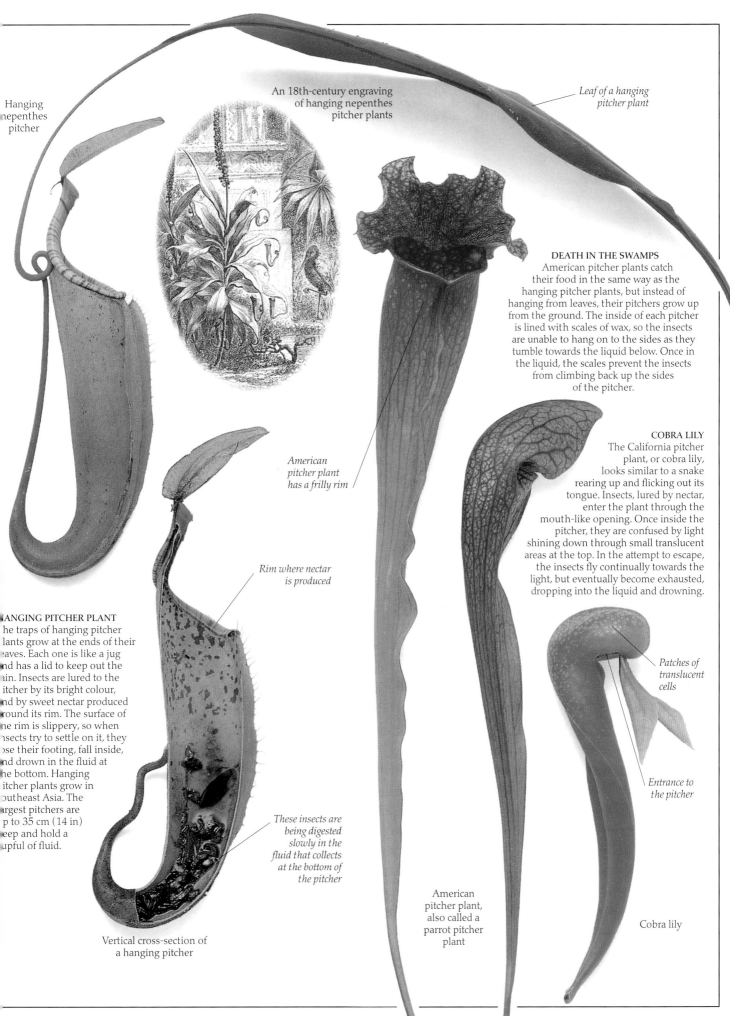

Hanging
nepenthes
pitcher

An 18th-century engraving
of hanging nepenthes
pitcher plants

*Leaf of a hanging
pitcher plant*

DEATH IN THE SWAMPS
American pitcher plants catch
their food in the same way as the
hanging pitcher plants, but instead of
hanging from leaves, their pitchers grow up
from the ground. The inside of each pitcher
is lined with scales of wax, so the insects
are unable to hang on to the sides as they
tumble towards the liquid below. Once in
the liquid, the scales prevent the insects
from climbing back up the sides
of the pitcher.

COBRA LILY
The California pitcher
plant, or cobra lily,
looks similar to a snake
rearing up and flicking out its
tongue. Insects, lured by nectar,
enter the plant through the
mouth-like opening. Once inside the
pitcher, they are confused by light
shining down through small translucent
areas at the top. In the attempt to escape,
the insects fly continually towards the
light, but eventually become exhausted,
dropping into the liquid and drowning.

*American
pitcher plant
has a frilly rim*

*Rim where nectar
is produced*

*Patches of
translucent
cells*

HANGING PITCHER PLANT
The traps of hanging pitcher
plants grow at the ends of their
leaves. Each one is like a jug
and has a lid to keep out the
rain. Insects are lured to the
pitcher by its bright colour,
and by sweet nectar produced
around its rim. The surface of
the rim is slippery, so when
insects try to settle on it, they
lose their footing, fall inside,
and drown in the fluid at
the bottom. Hanging
pitcher plants grow in
Southeast Asia. The
largest pitchers are
up to 35 cm (14 in)
deep and hold a
cupful of fluid.

*These insects are
being digested
slowly in the
fluid that collects
at the bottom of
the pitcher*

*Entrance to
the pitcher*

Vertical cross-section of
a hanging pitcher

American
pitcher plant,
also called a
parrot pitcher
plant

Cobra lily

41

Caught in a trap

To an unwary insect, the unusually shaped tip of a Venus flytrap leaf appears most inviting. Not only is the insect attracted by what looks like a safe landing place, it is also tempted by the promise of food in the form of nectar. But it is all a trick. As soon as the insect settles, the leaf-tip springs to life with lightning speed. Within a second, the hapless insect finds itself trapped, as the two halves of the leaf-tip snap shut. There is a second, slower phase of closure after the plant has tested what it has caught using sensory glands on the upper surface of the leaf-tip. If the prey contains protein, the trap closes fully, and digestion begins. The traps of the Venus flytrap are formed by two kidney-shaped lobes at the tip of the leaf, with a hinge formed by the midrib. The whole of the leaf is green and therefore able to photosynthesize (pp.14–15). Large bristles on the upper surface of the trap work like triggers with a clever device. If just one bristle is touched, by a raindrop for example, the trap stays open. But if two or more bristles are touched in quick succession, it quickly shuts to catch its victim.

A MOST HORRIBLE TORTURE
Like the Venus flytrap, humans have also been known to inflict a frightful and lingering death on their victims, as this rather gruesome engraving shows.

Marginal teeth

Trigger bristle

Damselfly touches the trigger bristles

Damselfly is caught in the closing trap

Midrib of leaf

Leaf-tip shaped like a kidney

Lower part of the leaf

Open trap

1 THE TRAP IS TRIGGERED
A damselfly lands on the trap and touches the trigger bristles on the trap's upper surface. Initially, special cells in the hinge, called motor cells, are filled with liquid. As soon as the triggers are fired, this liquid rushes out of the motor cells, making them collapse. This causes the trap to spring shut. The damselfly either does not notice this movement, or reacts too slowly.

2 CLOSING UP
After about one-fifth of a second, the sides of the trap are already closing over their victim. Because the marginal teeth point slightly outwards, they help to make sure that the insect does not fall out as the trap shuts. Even if it has sensed danger, it is now too late for the damselfly to make its escape.

After one-fifth of a second

GROWING A FLYTRAP

The first living specimen of the Venus flytrap arrived in England from America in the mid-18th century. Never before had such an unusual and spectacular plant been seen live in Europe, and it aroused great curiosity among botanists. Today, Venus flytraps can be grown as pot plants. Because they come from waterlogged bogs with slightly acid soil, they must never be allowed to dry out and are best planted in peat. It is important to water them with distilled water, because tap water often contains dissolved minerals that will reduce the plant's chances of survival. Venus flytraps do produce clusters of white flowers, but this does not often happen with indoor specimens, especially if they are fed frequently with insects.

*n early
9th-century
ainting of
e Venus
ytrap by
edoute, who
ainted the
ants kept by
e Empress
osephine at
almaison
.61)*

Flower stem

*pen
ap*

A WATERY HABITAT

Venus flytraps come from the bogs of North Carolina in the eastern United States. Each plant grows from a small rhizome, and produces several traps. Each trap can catch about three insects before it withers.

FLOATING TRAPS

This waterwheel plant is a small water plant that belongs to the same family of plants as the Venus flytrap and the sundews. Its leaves end in small traps that catch tiny water animals. They can close in one-fiftieth of a second.

Marginal teeth close around the damselfly

Marginal teeth form a cage around the damselfly

3 COMING TOGETHER

After two-fifths of a second, the marginal teeth have almost met. They are arranged alternately, so that they do not crash into each other as the trap closes. Meanwhile, inside the trap, the trigger bristles fold back. This ensures that they are not damaged and will be able to work again when the trap reopens.

The trap is almost closed

4 ALL EXITS SEALED

When the trap shuts, its sides remain at a slight angle to each other. At this stage, very small insects can climb out between the marginal teeth, but the damselfly is too big and is securely held in. The trap would be wasted on small insects, as it can digest only two or three insects before it becomes ineffective. After 30 minutes the sides of the trap will close fully and the plant will begin to digest its prisoner.

5 DIGESTION

Special glands inside the trap secrete acid and substances called enzymes, which will slowly digest all the soft parts of the insect's body. These glands later absorb the digested insect. It will take about two weeks for the damselfly to be fully digested, and for the trap to be ready for another meal. When the trap re-opens, the insect's hard exoskeleton, which includes the wings, will be blown away on the breeze.

After two-fifths of a second

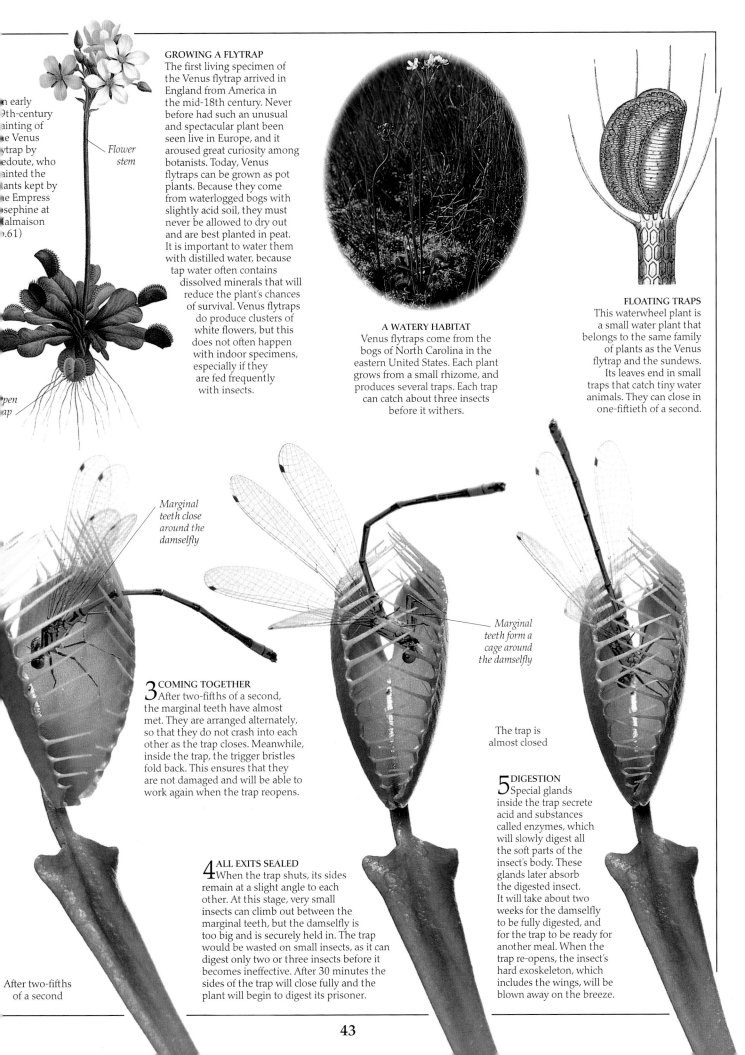

Parasitic plants

Giant rafflesia flower

PARASITIC PLANTS ARE CHEATS. Rather than making their own food using the energy from sunlight, they have developed a means of stealing the food made by other plants, known as host plants. Because they do not need sunlight, many parasitic plants spend most of their lives hidden from sight. They attach themselves to the stems or roots of their host plants by means of suckers, known as haustoria. The haustoria penetrate the host's food channels and absorb the sugars and minerals that the parasitic plant needs to live. The world of parasitic plants is a complicated one. Some plants, such as mistletoe and the eyebrights, are only partly parasitic and are known as hemiparasites. These plants have green leaves, so they can use the Sun's energy to make some food for themselves.

OLD TRADITION
The custom of kissing under mistletoe may be older than you think, for this plant was sacred to the ancient British priests known as the Druids some 2,000 years ago.

Giant sepals unfold as the flower opens

THE STINKING GIANT
The world's heaviest flower is a species of rafflesia, a parasite that lives on the roots of vines in the jungles of southeast Asia. Each flower weighs nearly 7 kg (15 lb), and reaches up to 1 m (3 ft) in diameter. The flower fills the air with a putrid smell that attracts pollinating flies. This plant is the largest of 50 species, all of them completely parasitic.

Sepals are thick and fleshy

MAKING A BREAK-IN
Dodder stems spread over their hosts looking like lengths of tangled string. These stems develop haustoria that penetrate their host's food channels. Young dodders have roots to help them become established, but as they grow the roots wither away.

Dodder flowers

Dodder stem twisting around the stem of its host plant

Dodder flowers

Haustoria penetrating the stem of its host

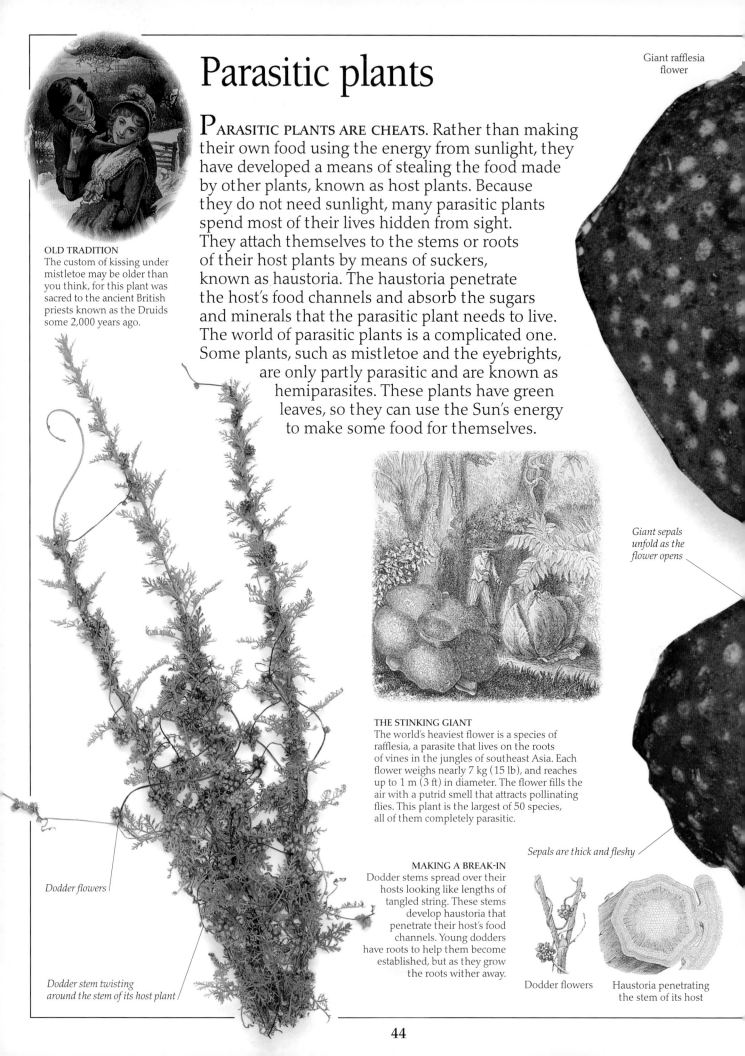

Plant passengers

NOT ALL PLANTS that live on others are parasites (pp.44–45). In fact, many more of them are simply passengers that grow on larger plants, such as trees, without causing them any harm. Such plants are described as epiphytic, and many of them can get all the water they need simply by absorbing it from the air, or by collecting it in structures formed for the purpose. They collect minerals by extracting them from trickling rainwater and plant debris. Being an epiphyte gives a small plant a chance to collect a lot of light without the need for tall stems. So successful is this way of life that few trees are without their passengers. In cool parts of the world, epiphytes are usually small, simple plants such as algae, lichens, and mosses. But in moist regions close to the equator, they are much larger. As well as the plants that spend their entire lives up in the trees, there are others that start or end their lives in this way. Some creeping plants, known as stranglers, germinate on trees and then become rooted in the soil. Others climb up on to plants but then their roots wither away, leaving them perched high up near the light.

FOREST CLIMBERS
These large, woody climbers, known as lianas, grow in the forests of Central America.

Leaves have a special coating to reduce water loss

High up in the trees it is easier for plants to collect enough light

HIGH-RISE FLOWERS
In the forests of Sri Lanka, epiphytic orchids can be found growing on the trees. Most epiphytic plants live in tropical and subtropical forests, because they require humid conditions.

THE BROMELIAD'S PRIVATE POND
Bromeliads are a family of plants that includes the pineapple. Many bromeliads grow on other plants. Instead of collecting water with long, aerial roots like orchids, they channel rainwater into a central reservoir (right) with their stiff, spiky leaves. Hairs on the leaves then absorb the water so the plant can use it. A big bromeliad holds over 5 litres (1 gallon) of water, and provides a home for water animals such as tree-frog tadpoles.

A species of
moth orchid

EPIPHYTIC ORCHIDS
There are up to 25,000 species of orchid
in the world. Many tropical orchids live by
perching on other plants. Orchid seeds are
tiny, and a single plant may produce a
million of them. The wind blows the seeds
of epiphytic species on to the bark of trees,
where they can germinate. Each of these
perching orchids has three types of aerial
root: for clinging to the host; for absorbing
minerals; and for extracting water from the
atmosphere. Some epiphytic orchids store
water and food reserves in swollen stems
known as pseudobulbs.

*Flowers produce
minute seeds to be
dispersed by wind*

*Thick, trailing
aerial roots
collect moisture,
as well as
minerals from
trickling
rainwater*

*Tarzan used lianas
to swing from tree to
tree across the
jungle*

Entwined
liana stems

*Liana stems
make a
natural rope*

NATURAL ROPES
Lianas are climbing plants with
flexible woody stems. Sometimes
they twine around each other for
mutual support. If the original
support dies and decays, the
lianas are left suspended from
the forest canopy. Other plants,
called stranglers, start life above
ground and then grow roots
downwards. Their roots form a
mesh around the trunks of trees
and eventually kill the support.

Tarzan, a
fictional hero of
books, movies,
and comics

Adapting to water

THE FIRST PLANTS ON EARTH evolved in water. Today, water still teems with microscopic plants that have changed little from those distant ancestors. But aquatic flowering plants have a different history. Their ancestors originally left water and evolved on land, but as time has gone by they have returned to the watery habitat. Only a few flowering plants, such as the eel-grasses, live in the sea. Far more plant species live in ponds, lakes, and rivers. Most of them are rooted to the bottom, but some have no roots and receive all the nutrients they need from the water instead of the soil. Some water plants are not often noticed, because they spend all their lives under water. Species like the water lilies are more obvious, because their leaves float on the surface. Plants such as reeds and rushes form a group known as emergent plants. They grow up out of the water and often form thick beds at the water's edge.

Glossy yellow flowers

**LEAVIN
THE WATE**
The great
spearwort is a
emergent wat
plant. It starts i
annual cycle
growth und
water, but quick
reaches th
surface. T
flowers bloo
about 60 cm (2
above the wat
where they attra
pollinating insect

Greater
spearwort

HISTORIC HIDEOUT
The Bible tells how Pharaoh's daughter discovered the infant Moses hidden among bulrushes in the River Nile.

Spear-shaped leaves

UNDERWATER LEAVES
Fanwort has finely divided underwater leaves, which are not damaged by the current.

Fanwort

Victorian engraving of papyrus growing by the River Nile in Egypt

FLOATING ON THE SURFACE
When young, the leaves of water lilies are rolled up under water like short tubes. In spring, the leaves reach the surface, where they open out and lie flat to form pads. In some ponds and lakes, water lilies and other plants with floating leaves can completely cover the water's surface, robbing submerged plants of the light they need to survive. The leaves are tough and leathery, so water easily runs off their surface.

PLANT FOR PAPER
Papyrus is a giant reed that grows up to 3 m (9 ft) high. The ancient Egyptians discovered that the pith in the middle of its stems could be used to make a material for writing on – the very first paper.

Tough, waxy surface repels water

Flowers bloom above the water

Flexible stalks attach the leaves to the roots, which are anchored in the muddy bottom

AMAZONIAN GIANT
The floating leaves of the Amazonian water lily can reach a diameter of more than 2 m (6 ft).

Water lily

Surviving above the snowline

THE HIGHER THE ALTITUDE at which a plant grows, the colder the temperatures it has to endure. Very low temperatures create specific problems for plant life. Thin mountain air holds little heat, and on exposed mountainsides, strong winds create a chill factor that makes the cold even more penetrating. In addition, low rainfall and thin, frozen soils mean that water is scarce. However, many plants manage to survive despite the harsh conditions. In the Himalayas of Asia, flowering plants have been found at more than 6,000 m (20,000 ft), sheltering in hollows in the frost-shattered rock. These plants, called alpine plants, are typically small and compact, so they can survive on the high mountain peaks, or in the frozen polar regions. Alpine plants often grow in dense cushions or flattened mats, giving protection against the cold, drying wind. Upright, spreading branches would be battered by the wind, and large leaves would lose valuable heat and water.

Precariously perched tent of an alpine plant collector

TOUGH WORK
Alpine plant collectors must be fit enough to scale the heights, and prepared to endure tough conditions at high altitude.

Mountain avens

Mountain kidney vetch

QUICK WORK
When spring comes, the mountain slopes burst into colour as alpine plants begin to flower. In high mountain areas where the summers are short, these plants have to flower and produce seeds quickly before winter comes around again.

HAIRY LEAVES
Mountain avens are plants that grow on high ground, from the Alps of Europe to the Arctic. Fine hairs on the undersides of their leaves minimize water loss and protect against the cold.

BUILT-IN SUNSCREENS
This mountain kidney vetch grows high in the Alps, and has leaves covered in hairs. Like those of the silversword, they protect the leaves from Sun damage, reduce water loss, and act as insulation.

Dwarf hebe

RADIATION HAZARD
The sunlight that falls on high mountain tops in the tropics is more intense than anywhere else on Earth. The silversword grows in Hawaii, US, at altitudes of up to 4,000 m (15,000 ft). Its leaves are covered with fine white hairs that protect the plant from much of the Sun's dangerous ultraviolet radiation.

PLANT CUSHIONS
This dwarf hebe from New Zealand is an evergreen plant with small tough leaves that can withstand sharp frost. It grows in dense cushions that trap heat, prevent wind damage, and reduce water loss. These cushions are covered in white flowers every spring.

50

**FLAT
AGAINST
THE GROUND**
Many alpine plants
spread over the
ground in the form
of flat mats, keeping
out of the path of icy
winds. *Mazus reptans*
is a mat-forming plant
from the Himalayas.

*Mazus
reptans*

Garland
flower

A MINIATURE SHRUB
This alpine daphne,
or garland flower, is a
shrub in miniature. Larger
daphnes grow at lower levels.

Alpine
moltkias

SMALL LEAVES
Moltkias are members
of the forget-me-not
family. Unlike many
of their lowland
relatives, alpine
moltkias have small
leaves, which are
better able to withstand
strong mountain winds.

MOUNDS OF COLOUR
Like many alpine plants, this
beautiful phlox from North
America has brilliantly coloured
flowers. They stand out against
the rocky slopes and attract
pollinating insects.

Alpine
phlox

Rock rose

DUAL PROTECTION
Mountain rock roses
are protected from the
weather in two ways.
The bushy plants are
able to stand up to strong
winds better than those
with taller, more rigid
stems. Their leaves and
stems are covered with
fine hairs that act as
insulation at night.

TWO WAYS TO SPREAD
This species of storksbill
lives in the high Pyrenees of
Europe. It spreads both with
seeds and with its creeping
root system (p.32).

MOUNTAIN DWARF
Many mountain
plants that survive at
great heights, such as this
St John's wort, are much
smaller than their
lowland relatives.

St John's
wort

Storksbill

51

Living without water

No PLANT CAN LIVE entirely without water. But in very dry regions, where water is scarce, plants called cacti and succulents are able to survive for a number of years between rainstorms. In the world's driest places, rain often comes in irregular but heavy bursts, so the plants that live there have evolved ways of collecting as much water as possible during downpours. The water is then stored in preparation for the next drought. Many cacti and succulents have very long roots. Most of these roots grow near the surface, so that when it rains the plants can collect water from a wide area. Once the water is inside the plant, it is kept there by a number of special adaptations. Plants normally lose water from pores, called stomata, in the surface of their leaves. The plant can control these pores, and it will close them if it begins to lose too much water. Many cacti and succulents open the pores only at night, when the air is cool and less water can evaporate. Some of these plants have got around the problem of water loss by losing their leaves altogether.

Fish-hook cactus

Barrel cactus

Hedgeh[og] cactu[s]

Many cacti have beautiful flowers

Cross-section of square stem

THE CACTUS FAM[ILY]
Almost all true cacti come from [the] Americas. Because they live in v[ery] dry places, they have had to evo[lve] strange shapes to be able to surv[ive]. Most cacti have very thick stems a[nd] thick groups of spines instead [of] normal leaves. These spines m[ay] protect the plant from heat and c[old] as well as from attack by anim[als]. Many cacti have ridges down th[eir] stems to allow them to expand a[nd] store water when it rai[ns].

SIMILAR SHAPES FOR SIMILAR LIFESTYLES
Not all the spiny plants that live in dry places are cacti. The cactus-like plant on the far left is actually a spurge, a plant quite unrelated to the two cacti to its right. Like the cacti, it has lost its leaves and developed a tough, water-holding stem. This is a typical example of convergent evolution, in which plants or animals in similar environments have evolved in similar ways.

Row of spines

Clusters of spines

Spurge

Prickly pear cactus

Cleistocactus

Cross-section of round stem

THE GIANT SAGUARO
The saguaro is one of the world's tallest cacti. A 250-year-old plant can be 20 m (60 ft) high and can weigh 6 tonnes.

Succulents

Plants with fleshy leaves or stems for storing water are known as succulents. They include the group of plants called cacti. There are three main types of succulent. Stem succulents, such as cacti, store water in their stems, and tend to live in the driest climates. Leaf succulents, some of which are shown on this page, store water in their leaves, and grow in damper conditions. Finally, root succulents have thickened roots that serve as water reservoirs.

Cotyledon

Blue echeveria

The leaves of this species of Cotyledon *are fleshy, with a waxy surface, to reduce water loss*

The whitish, waxy coating on the surface of the leaves of Senecio antandroi *protects the plant from the harsh rays of the Sun*

LEAF SUCCULENTS
Leaf succulent plants live in semi-desert and also in salt marshes, where the salty conditions mean that fresh water has to be carefully conserved. Their leaves wrinkle up in prolonged dry weather. When it rains, they swell again as the plant takes in water.

Senecio antandroi

The plump leaves of Haworthia cymbiformis *are swollen with stored water*

Blue echeveria

Haworthia cymbiformis

Panda plant

The necklace vine gets its name from its leaves, which look as if they have been threaded on a string

Necklace vine

Panda plant

Senecio antandroi

Cotyledon

Necklace vine

LEAVES THAT WITHSTAND DROUGHT
As much as nine-tenths of the weight of a succulent leaf may be stored water. To conserve this vital store, the leaves have a waxy surface that hinders transpiration, which is the process by which leaves lose water. Some succulent leaves have a woolly surface that helps to keep the leaf cool, which in turn reduces water loss. Succulent leaves have evolved in many unrelated plant species throughout the dry regions of the world.

FLEETING FLOWERS
Many desert plants are ephemerals. This means that they germinate only after rain, and then complete their life cycle very rapidly. For a few days after rain, the desert is ablaze with their flowers. This sea of little yellow flowers is made up of thousands of sand sunflowers, which have all come into bloom at once in the Utah Desert, US.

Food from plants

PLANTS HAVE BEEN CULTIVATED as food crops for thousands of years. The earliest humans lived in nomadic groups, roaming the landscape in search of food. Eventually, these peoples settled down, and instead of collecting plant foods from the wild they began to cultivate them. When the time came to gather seeds to produce crops for the following year, they tended to take seeds from the healthiest plants. As they did this year after year, they began to produce better crop plants. Later, more deliberate efforts were made to improve crops by selecting and cultivating the strongest plants, and this process is continuing today. As farming settlements were established independently in different parts of the world, so different crops were cultivated in each place. This meant that when early travellers first visited distant continents, they found many new and exciting foods to bring home. The crops we eat today come from many different parts of the world.

MARKET IN PERU
Potatoes originated in the high Andes of South America. Many varieties of potato are still grown there, as this market scene shows.

KEPT IN THE DARK
If allowed to grow in the light, chicory has a bitter taste. To reduce this bitterness, the plant is cut back to the ground and then allowed to regrow with almost no light. The pale, blanched leaves of the new chicory shoot are far less bitter. If cultivated chicory were grown entirely in the light, the plant would look very similar to wild chicory.

Primitive form of corn plant and cob

Blanched shoot of cultivated chicory

Modern corn cob

Wild chicory

PRIMITIVE CORN
Maize is a cereal: like wheat and rice, it is a member of the grass family. It was first cultivated in Central America, and some primitive forms of maize can still be found growing there. As a result of selective breeding, the size and shape of the modern corn cob have been increased.

Fruits of a wild
tomato, from
Mexico

*Wild cabbage has
dark green,
leathery leaves*

The wild cabbage
grows near the sea. It
has leathery leaves,
loosely arranged on a
branched stem. Years
of breeding have got
rid of the plant's
bitter taste, and made
its leaves more juicy.
The shape of the
plant has also
changed so that, in
most cultivated
cabbages, the leaves
are packed tightly
together. In red
cabbage varieties,
certain natural
pigments have been
built up as a result of
selective breeding.

Wild tomato
flowers

*Cultivated
tomato flowers
are very similar*

Cultivated
tomatoes

*tivated tomatoes
e become
h bigger
ugh
ding*

BIGGER – AND BETTER?
The tomato's wild ancestor is a
red berry the size of a small grape.
It is much sweeter than a modern
tomato, with a stronger flavour.

GROWING IN WATER
Rice, which was cultivated in the Far
East at least 5,000 years ago, forms the
staple cereal diet of over one half of
the world's population. It usually grows
in fields of standing water, known as
paddy fields.

*Flower
head of
wild carrot*

Working in
the paddy fields

Modern
cabbage

*Wild
carrot
root*

Cultivated
carrot

Modern
red cabbage

DIBLE ROOTS
he wild carrot is found all over
urope and through much of
sia, but its roots are white or
ly slightly coloured. Only in
ghanistan is there a variety of
ild carrot with orange roots. The
rrot was probably first cultivated
that region, and then introduced
other parts of the world.

CARROTS AND CABBAGES
This detail from a 16th-century
painting by the Dutch artist Lucas
Van Valkenborch proves that even
400 years ago there was a wide
variety of vegetables available.

The story of wheat

FOOD FOR THE MASSES
People have grown cereals for food for thousands of years, as this picture from the 11th century shows.

WHEAT HAS BEEN CULTIVATED by humans as a valuable source of food for at least 9,000 years. Grains of wheat have been found preserved in ancient Egyptian tombs, and it is known that it was the chief cereal of the ancient Greeks and Romans. The cultivation of wheat originated in the region known as the Fertile Crescent, which includes part of modern-day Israel, Turkey, Iraq, and Iran. Once a rich farming area, today much of it is desert. Wheat is now grown in most parts of the world, and the quality has improved greatly. The early, primitive species, such as einkorn and emmer, had long, thin stalks that were easily broken in bad weather. Their small grains meant that a large number of plants only produced a relatively low yield of grain. Today, as a result of extensive breeding programmes, better varieties have been found that have higher yields, resist drought, and withstand disease.

CUTTING THE CORN
Wild grasses drop their ripe seeds. The first farmers selected plants that held on to the seeds, so that the grain could be harvested.

Grains of wild einkorn

Grains emm

WILD EINKORN
This wild grass is probably one of the ancestors of all cultivated wheats. It has long, thin stalks and small heads and grains.

EINKORN
This early wheat species is still grown in parts of Turkey for animal feed. Its small grains are difficult to thresh.

WILD EMMER
This wild grass is the ancestor of emmer, another primitive wheat. The heads and grains are larger than those of einkorn.

EMMER
Emmer was the chief cereal in ancient Greek and Roman times. It is one of the ancestors of modern cultivated wheat varieties.

[SPE]LT

[Th]e great leap forward for wheats
[cam]e when emmer crossed, or
[hyb]ridized, with wild goat grass
[tha]t was growing as a weed in
[wh]eat fields. The result was
[spe]lt wheat, which is still
[cul]tivated in parts of
[nor]thwest Europe.

Spelt grains

*The long, spiky
bristles attached to
scales around each
grain are called awns*

WHEATFIELD PRAIRIE
Today's wheat is much shorter
than that of a century ago.
Breeders have reduced
the amount of stalk, so
that the plant does not
bend over, making
it difficult to harvest
the grain. This is an
important step
forward for the major
grain-producing countries
of the world, where vast
areas of wheat are grown.

*Brown bread
baked with
unbleached
wholemeal
flour*

Durum wheat

Pasta
shells

DURUM WHEAT
Another large-grain
wheat closely related
to emmer is durum,
or macaroni,
wheat. It is grown
widely today to
provide the flour
for pasta and
biscuits. Because its
gluten content is low,
it does not make
good bread. Modern
durum wheat has
bigger grains as a
result of intensive
breeding.

*Uncooked
wholemeal flour*

*Grains of
bread wheat*

Bread
wheat

BREAD WHEAT
Bread wheat is also a hybrid of emmer
and wild goat grass, and it is the most
widely grown modern wheat. Its large
grains have a high gluten content,
which makes bread dough elastic and
enables light, airy bread to be made.

*White bread,
made from very
finely ground flour
that has been bleached*

Potions and poisons

IN ANCIENT TIMES, plants were the main source of medicines. By trial and error, it was discovered that particular species could cure certain diseases. These plants were often grown in special gardens, and their details noted in books called herbals. Today, many plants are still used by the pharmaceutical industry. The chemicals they produce may be poisonous in large quantities, but small amounts can prove very useful in the treatment of some illnesses. The search for new medicines continues today, and every year pharmacologists examine thousands of plants from all over the world.

MANDRAKE
The mandrake root, once used in medicines, sometimes looks almost human. It was usually pulled up by a dog, because, according to an old superstition, the root would shriek as it came out of the ground. Any human who heard the noise would die.

Aloe vera

Cosmetic preparation made from aloe vera

Jojoba

COSMETIC EFFECT
Plants are often used in cosmetics for their pleasant smell, or soothing oils. Two plants that are popular in today's cosmetics are jojoba and aloe vera. Both live in dry places and contain oils that help to keep skin soft.

OUT OF THE EAST
In China, ginseng has been prized for about 5,000 years. The powdered root has a stimulant effect, and can aid recovery from illness. Ginseng is grown commercially and is now sold all over the world.

Red ginseng root from Korea

THE OPIUM POPP
For thousands of years opiu poppies have been grown as source of drugs. Raw opiur is the poppy's dried sar It oozes out of the unrip seed head after it ha been scarred with knife. Opium is use in the manufacture o morphine, codein and heroin – drug that can be dead if misuse

Opium poppies growing in Turkey

Beans contain oil and poisonous ricin

Detail of a page from a 12th-century herbal

A gieuf iquidem dr ocofindos
Quidamucamellam eam uoc

A DEADLY DOSE
The oil from the beans of the castor-oil plant has been used to purify the system since the days of the ancient Egyptians. The beans also contain ricin, one of the most potent poisons known. Ricin is so powerful that, if eaten, just one bean is enough to kill an adult.

Castor-oil plant

Leaves of
the dumb
cane

THE DUMB CANE
The name of this plant comes
from its poisonous sap. If
this is swallowed, it
makes the mouth
swell so much that
talking becomes
difficult.

DRINK OR DRUG?
The mescal cactus contains a
hallucinogenic substance called
mescaline, which is used in the
religious rituals of certain Mexican
Indian tribes. Confusingly, the
drink mescal (or mezcal) is not
derived from the mescal cactus,
but from the agave plant,
which is also native
to Mexico.

Mescal
cactus

Mescal,
a drink made
from the
agave plant

DEADLY BERRIES
The drug atropine, which is used in
eye surgery and to treat stomach
complaints, is derived from
a very poisonous plant
called belladonna, or
deadly nightshade.

FROM COCA TO COCAINE
Many centuries ago, South
American Indians discovered
that chewing the leaves of the
coca plant dulled pain and
prevented tiredness. Coca
leaves contain the drug
cocaine. Although a
valuable anaesthetic,
cocaine can be
dangerously
addictive.

Coca leaves for sale

oca leaves

Foxglove

Drinking gin and
tonic water in India,
at the end of the
19th century

Belladonna,
or deadly
nightshade

ELP FOR
HE HEART
he leaves of the
oxglove contain a
ubstance that is
sed to treat heart
nditions. In large
ses, it produces
lpitations and
zziness, but in
naller doses, it helps
e heart to beat more
owly and strongly.

A CURE FOR MALARIA
Quinine, which is used in the
treatment of malaria, is obtained
from the bark of South American
cinchona trees. Quinine is also used as
a bitter flavour in tonic water, a drink
that is commonly mixed with gin.

Cinchona
leaves

The plant collectors

MANY OF THE PLANTS that have become common in gardens all over the world are, in fact, very far from home. Most fuchsias, for example, come originally from South America, wisteria from China and Japan, many azaleas from the Himalayas in Asia, and tulips from western and central Asia. These are just some of the thousands of plants that have been carried across the world by plant collectors. Plant collecting had its heyday in the 19th and early 20th centuries, as intrepid botanists travelled farther and farther afield in search of unknown plants. Some collectors experienced great hardships on their voyages to distant places – they were shot at, caught in earthquakes, and attacked by wild animals. But despite all such adversities, the lure of making new discoveries spurred them on to explore some of the world's most remote and dangerous places.

A 19th-century plant collector with his collecting case, or vasculum

Scutellaria tournefortia

This plant is named after its discoverer, Joseph Pitton de Tournefort

ROYAL MISSION
Joseph Pitton de Tournefort (1656–1708) was a botanist who was sent to the eastern Mediterranean by the French king Louis XIV. He returned with the specimens and seeds of over a thousand plants, many of which became garden favourites.

A 19th-century vasculum containing *Sarcococca hookeriana*, a species of sweet box

GOING EAST
The picture above shows botanists on a plant-collecting expedition to China in the 1920s. This region of the world has been of great interest to botanists for many years, and expeditions made there today still discover new plant species. The photograph on the right shows a botanist at work on a modern plant-collecting expedition.

Sarcococca hookeriana is named after the Hookers

FATHER AND SON
William Hooker (1785–1865) and his son Joseph (1817–1911) were both passionately interested in plants. William Hooker became the first director of The Royal Botanic Gardens at Kew in England. Joseph is especially remembered for collecting many species of rhododendron in the Himalayas.

Leaves of the
plane tree

Tradescant
father
and son

GOING WEST
John Tradescant and his son, also named John,
were English plantsmen. Tradescant the Elder
collected in Russia, and Tradescant the Younger
collected in America. The younger Tradescant
imported trees into Europe. These included the
tulip tree and the western plane.

FIT FOR ROYALTY
Plant collecting is an ancient pursuit. This
Egyptian mural shows the earliest recorded
expedition, which took place in 1495 BCE.
Collectors brought back frankincense trees for
Queen Hatshepsut from the Horn of Africa.

Tradescantia – a border
plant named after John
Tradescant the Elder

Beautifully preserved
botanical reference books

THE EMPRESS COLLECTOR
Empress Josephine, the wife of
Napoleon, created a unique garden at
her house at Malmaison, with roses
brought from all around the world.
At the time, France was at war with
Britain, but ships carrying the imperial
roses were allowed safe passage.

Plant
collectors

Looking at plant

THERE ARE TWO TYPES of pla
collection – living plants and preserv
specimens. A herbarium is a collection
preserved specimens, usually pressed, th
can be examined by botanists. Collections
living plants are equally important, and sometim
ensure that rare plant species do not die out. Maki
your own collection of flowers and pressing them i
good way to learn about plants. However, you shou
not pick flowers that are growing wild in the countrysi
as this prevents them from producing seeds. All wild flow
species are protected by law, and you must not uproot the
without receiving permission from the person who owns the lar
If you want to try to grow your own plants, you can collect sm
amounts of seed, or you can buy wild flower seeds produced by pla
that have been raised in nurseries. Growing your own
plants gives you a chance to study them
without harming plants in the wild.

Herbarium
specimen
sheet

Preserving
bottle

HERB. HORT. REG. B

Na echinacea

Forest, Lincs

Box
containing
dried specimen

4787
HERB. HORT. BOT. REG. KEW.

Dendrobium (lindleyi) aggregatum R.d.

Thailand

Menzies & July
89

Plant press

BOTANIST'S COLLECTING EQUIPMENT
When collecting plants for the herbarium,
a specimen is pressed and then mounted
on a herbarium sheet with a label saying
where and when it was found. The
herbarium sheet can then be
consulted by botanists wishing
to study the plant in detail.

Secateurs

Trowel

Sketch pad

LEARNING MORE ABOUT PLANTS
One of the best ways of finding out
more about wild flowers is to draw or
photograph them. If you draw them,
you will notice many details about
their structure, which will help you to
identify the plant family. A magnifying
glass is very useful for examining
leaves and petals more closely.
Collecting seeds and growing plants
from them requires patience and care.
Stored seeds should always be kept
dry. Many seeds will germinate better
if they are left in a refrigerator for a
few weeks before planting. This cold
period simulates the low winter
temperatures they may experience in
the wild. Large seeds, like those from
sweet peas, germinate more quickly
if they are first scratched, or
scarified, with sandpaper.

Magnifying glass

Scissors

Camera

Envelopes for
collecting seeds

PRESERVING SPECIMENS
Plants can be pressed with a simple screw
press. The specimens are laid between two
sheets of absorbent paper, which should be
changed for dry sheets every day or so. It can
take several weeks for specimens to dry out.

Base of
screw
press

Simple
screw press

Top of
screw
press

Screws for
tightening
the press

Did you know?

AMAZING FACTS

Bristlecone pine tree

The oldest seed known to botany comes from the North American Arctic lupine plant and is thought to be about 10,000 years old. The tendency of lupine seeds to be naturally preserved by the cold gave scientists the idea to place seeds in cold storage as stock for the future.

The fynbos, or evergreen bushland, of the Cape region in South Africa contains one of the world's most dense concentrations of plant species within a small area. The eastern and northern coasts around Cape Town are home to an amazing range of aloes, proteas, and ericas. There are an estimated 6,500 plant species in this tiny region. This is almost as many as in the whole of the continent of Europe.

Sphagnum moss, which is found in bogs and contributes to the formation of peat, can soak up more than 25 times its own dry weight in moisture.

As plants get smaller we know less about them. Scientists estimate that they have identified 85–90 per cent of flowering plants, but only about 5 per cent of the world's microscopic organisms.

The largest fruit is the pumpkin, which can weigh up to 513 kg (1,130 lb). Its close rival is the squash, which has been known to grow to 405 kg (893 lb).

The main ingredient in chocolate is the bean of the cacao tree, which grows in the rainforests of South America.

The oldest individual living plant (as opposed to a clump) is thought to be a bristlecone pine (*Pinus longaeva*). Named Methusaleh, it is currently 4,900 years old. It lives in the White Mountains of California, United States, but its exact location is kept secret to protect it from harm.

The orchid family has more species than any other flowering plant, with 25,000–30,000 species recognized, mostly in tropical regions. Orchids are found in every continent except for Antarctica, inhabiting just about every type of environment, except for extreme deserts and salt water.

Arctic lupine

Fossils of the still-existing gingko tree (*Gingko biloba*) date back some 160 million years. It first appeared at the time of the dinosaurs, during the Jurassic period. Today, extract from the bark and root of the tree is considered to have medicinal benefits for humans. The seed kernel of the tree is a delicacy in China.

The raffia palm (*Raffia ruffia*) of Madagascar and Africa's tropical eastern coast has the world's largest leaves, measuring up to 20 m (66 ft) in length.

The banyan tree (*Ficus benghalensis*) has aerial roots that grow down from the tree's branches and eventually form new trunks. In this way, the banyan grows both upwards and downwards.

Japan greatly values the flower of the chrysanthemum, and includes its emblem on the national flag. The country has dedicated a whole day to the flower, September 9, and the *feng shui* tradition teaches that the chrysanthemum brings laughter and happiness to a home.

Tulips were originally native to Turkey, Iran, Syria, and parts of Asia, before being brought to Europe by travelling merchants in the 16th century. The Dutch were the first European nation to cultivate tulips, doing so in 1593. By 1633, the Dutch upper classes were so gripped by tulip mania that individual bulbs were changing hands for vast amounts of money.

A plant called St Mary's bean, from Central America, has the greatest known range for drifting seeds. Its seeds have been washed up in the Marshall Islands, in the Pacific Ocean, and also on the coast of Norway – places that are 24,150 km (15,000 miles) apart.

Proteas

Orchid

QUESTIONS AND ANSWERS

Red cherry fruits

Q Why are the fruits of the cherry plant red?

A The fruits of the cherry plant are bright red in colour to attract birds to eat the fruits. The cherry fruits contain seeds that have a hard protective covering. This ensures that when the seeds are eaten by birds they pass unharmed through the digestive system of the creatures. In this way, the seeds are safely spread, and the plant guarantees the survival of its offspring. Plants pollinated by insects are rarely red because insects, with the exception of butterflies, cannot see the colour red.

Q Which plant is considered to be the most bizarre of all?

A *Welwitschia mirabilis*, also known as the tumboa, from the Namib desert in Africa, is one of the strangest plants in the world. Known to live for up to 2,000 years, it has a stumpy stem and just two strap-like leaves, which grow non-stop throughout its life. As the plant ages, its leaves become twisted and gnarled, and they eventually can be many metres long. The leaves are tough and woody – an adaptation that helps to stop them being eaten, or drying out. *Welwitschia* survives in a region where there is little rain, but where fog rolls in from the sea. The plant's leaves gather moisture from the fog, helping it to survive. *Welwitschia* does not grow flowers, but produces seeds in cones.

Q What is the richest plant region of the world?

A South America, which holds an estimated 90,000 species, is the world's richest plant region. Brazil is the country with the greatest known number of plant species, at 56,000, followed by Colombia, with 35,000 species. Mexico, Venezuela, Ecuador, Bolivia, and Peru are not far behind. The proliferation of plant species in this part of the world is thought to be due to the moist habitat associated with its tropical rainforests, as well as the relatively recent arrival of humans.

Q Why do some tree leaves change colour in autumn?

A As the days become colder and shorter, chlorophyll, the green pigment in the leaves, breaks down and flows back into the tree. Meanwhile, waste products, such as tannins, pass out into the leaves. This chemical change produces browns and reds in the colours of the leaves as they die. Trees that lose their leaves are said to be deciduous.

Record Breakers

Smallest plant
• The world's smallest flowering plant is duckweed, (*Wolffia angusta*). A tablespoon can hold more than 100,000 plants, with each measuring only 0.8 mm (1/30 in) long and 0.4 mm (1/60 in) wide.

Largest seed
• The largest seed produced by any plant is that of the coco-de-mer (*Lodoicea maldivica*), from the Seychelles. This palm, also known as the double coconut tree, produces seeds that weigh up to 23 kg (50 lb) and take up to 10 years to grow into a tree.

Tallest tree
• The Mendocino coast redwood (*Sequoia sempervirens*) found in California, United States, is the world's tallest tree, reaching a maximum height of 112.01 m (367½ ft).

Duckweed

Weltwitschia mirabilis

Plant classification

Gingko

THE PLANT KINGDOM is divided into different groups and contains about 400,000 separate species that we know about. The majority of plant organisms belong to the flowering plant family, or angiosperms. Plants that have seeds but no flowers are called gymnosperms. The groups shown here cover all of the main plant classifications.

Liverwort

Most liverworts have leaves, but some are flat and leafless

GINGKO

The gingko, or maidenhair, tree is native to China. A gymnosperm, it is related to conifers, but it has many unusual features, which is why it is classified in a group of its own. Unlike most conifers, gingkos are deciduous, and have fan-shaped leaves.

MOSSES AND LIVERWORTS

Mosses and liverworts belong to a group called the bryophytes, which number 14,000 species. These small plants usually grow in shaded, damp places. They first appeared around 425 million years ago, and they contributed to the formation of coal and peat.

FLOWERING PLANTS

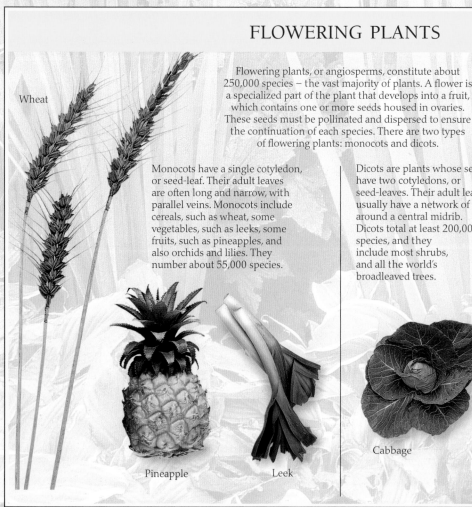

Wheat

Flowering plants, or angiosperms, constitute about 250,000 species – the vast majority of plants. A flower is a specialized part of the plant that develops into a fruit, which contains one or more seeds housed in ovaries. These seeds must be pollinated and dispersed to ensure the continuation of each species. There are two types of flowering plants: monocots and dicots.

Rose

Monocots have a single cotyledon, or seed-leaf. Their adult leaves are often long and narrow, with parallel veins. Monocots include cereals, such as wheat, some vegetables, such as leeks, some fruits, such as pineapples, and also orchids and lilies. They number about 55,000 species.

Dicots are plants whose seeds have two cotyledons, or seed-leaves. Their adult leaves usually have a network of veins around a central midrib. Dicots total at least 200,000 species, and they include most shrubs, and all the world's broadleaved trees.

Dicot plants often have woody stems

Pineapple

Leek

Cabbage

Cactus

Clubmoss

CLUBMOSSES

Clubmosses, or lycopodophytes, existed as far back as 430 million years ago. Today's clubmosses are small, with overlapping leaves and creeping stems, but some prehistoric clubmosses grew into giant trees. Clubmosses reproduce by growing spores.

ERNS

lso known as pteridophytes, ferns include around 12,000 species and rive in damp environments, such as forests. Fern leaves are called fronds, nd they carry spores on their underside. These spores produce tiny plants at reproduce in turn, giving rise to the next generation of adult ferns.

CYCADS

Cycads are gymnosperms that grow in tropical regions. Despite being similar in appearance to palms, they are not related to them. Cycads were abundant in the Jurassic Period (208–146 million years ago), but there are now just 100 species left. Their attractive leaves make them popular garden plants.

ONIFERS

his gymnosperm group of about 50 species comprises mostly rge evergreen trees. Conifers n photosynthesize even in inter, and they are often haracterized by leaves haped like needles. This roup includes pines, s, spruces, cedars, ypresses, and yews.

Pine

Cycad

HORSETAILS

These ancient plants are also called sphenophytes. Around 300 million years ago, they reached heights of 15 m (49 ft). Today there are only about 35 species left, most of which are under 1 m (3 ft) tall. This family is closely related to the fern group.

Vast horsetail forests once grew on Earth

Weltwitschia mirabilis, also known as the tumboa

GNETOPHYTES

Although they are gymnosperms, these cone-bearing desert plants resemble flowering plants in many ways. Gnetophytes were once thought to be a missing link between angiosperms and conifers. There are about 70 species.

Horsetail

Cones are produced during the summer months

Find out more

IF YOU WOULD LIKE TO find out more about plants, you won't have to search far. Indeed, you only have to look around you. Go exploring in your own garden or start growing a window box. Armed with a plant identification handbook, take a walk in your local park or countryside, where you will find plenty of specimens to admire and study. For more exotic species and a wealth of information, visit a botanical garden, or to check out ancient plant fossils, take a trip to a natural history museum. Flower markets can also be an interesting and colourful experience.

If an area of land is privately owned, always seek permission to visit from the owner

GO WILD
To see plants in a completely natural setting, just head for your local countryside (after informing an adult). Spring is a good time to observe budding flowers and new shoots. Few sights compare to the vivid beauty of a wild-flower meadow in midsummer bloom.

Wild flowers should not be plucked, as this disturbs the natural environment

BOTANICAL GARDENS
A botanical garden is dedicated to plants from around the world. Rare and exotic species are cultivated, often in specially controlled environments, such as greenhouses. Desert plants, for example, must be kept in a hot, dry climate for survival.

This garden pansy will lose some of its colour as it dries

Write the name of the plant and the date it was picked on the sheet of paper

COLLECTING DRIED FLOWERS
Pick a flower in full bloom. Detach the flower head and leaves and place them flat on a sheet of blotting paper. Fold and enclose the sheet between the pages of a heavy book, and leave the flower to dry out for a few weeks.

Places to visit

WOODLAND WALKS
There are many official countryside walks that choose specific routes best
suited to the time of year. The organized walk below follows a path that
takes ramblers through the first colourful crop of springtime bluebells.

ORNAMENTAL BUNCHES
A bouquet of flowers doesn't
have to fade away. Its beauty
can be preserved by taking it
out of water and keeping it in a
safe place until each stem has dried
out. Tie the bouquet with
a ribbon and display
it in a vase or on
the wall.

*This bunch of
dried flowers was
purchased at a
flower market*

IN YOUR OWN BACK YARD
If you have a garden, this is the best place to find out
more about plants. Using a notebook, you can log the
growth and development of various species through
the seasons. You can also grow your own plants.

ROOM WITH A VIEW
If you don't have access to a
garden, window boxes make
very rewarding miniature
gardens. Flowers and herbs
can be grown in any
container and placed on
a window ledge. Another
way to grow plants
outside is to cut an
opening in a large
bag of compost and
use it as a soil bed.

*Sunflower seeds
ideally should be
planted in May*

USEFUL WEBSITES

- Tropical plant database covering the incredible
  flora of the Amazon rainforest in South America:
  www.rain-tree.com/plants.htm
- The lowdown on botany for kids:
  **www.enchantedlearning.com/subjects/plants/
  glossary/**
- The Kew Gardens website has an online herbarium:
  www.kew.org/
- Garden tips from the Royal Horticultural Society:
  www.rhs.org.uk/index.asp

Glossary

ACHENE A dry, one-seeded fruit. All plants in the buttercup family have achenes.

ALGA A simple non-flowering plant that usually lives in water. Algae include seaweeds and many microscopic species.

ANGIOSPERM A flowering plant. Unlike gymnosperms, angiosperms grow their seeds inside a protective case called an ovary, which develops to form a fruit.

ANNUAL A plant that completes its life cycle within the growing season of one year.

Green alga, or seaweed

ANTHER The tip of a flower's stamen containing pollen.

AXIL The angle between the upper part of a stem and a leaf or branch. Buds develop in the axil.

AXIS The main stem or root in a plant.

BIENNIAL A plant that has two growing seasons. The seed is sown in the first year and flowers and fruits in its second year. The plant then dies.

BOTANY The scientific study of plants.

BRACT A small, leaf-like flap that grows just beneath a flower.

BUD The first visible sign of a new limb of a plant, or the protective case that encloses a flower that is still growing inside.

BULB An underground stem that stores food inside layers of fleshy scales. Most plants use bulbs to survive drought or cold.

Stem and leaves sprout from the bulb

BULBIL A small bud that grows into an independent plant.

BURR The prickly seed case of some plants.

CALYX The ring of sepals that protects a flower bud. The calyx often falls off when the flower blooms.

CARPEL The female organ of a flower. It consists of the stigma, the style, and the ovary.

Daffodil bulbs

CELL The smallest possible unit of living matter, visible only under a microscope. A cell consists of a nucleus surrounded by a fluid called cytoplasm, bounded by a cell wall.

CHLOROPHYLL The green pigment present in all plants and algae and involved in the process of photosynthesis.

CHLOROPLAST A microscopic green structure that contains chlorophyll, and which is found inside a plant cell. Chloroplasts capture energy from sunlight.

CLIMBER A plant that grows upwards and outwards, attaching itself to structures such as walls and fences.

COROLLA The ring of petals in a flower.

COTYLEDON A specialized leaf that is pre-packed inside a seed. Cotyledons often look quite different to ordinary leaves.

DECIDUOUS A plant that loses its leaves every autumn.

DICOT A plant whose seeds have two cotyledons (seed-leaves). The leaves of a dicot, or dicotyledon, are often broad, and they have veins arranged in a network.

EMBRYO A young plant in its earliest stages of development.

ENDOSPERM A supply of food that is stored inside a seed. The endosperm fuels the seedling's early growth.

EVERGREEN A plant that retains its leaves all year round, such as pines and firs.

FILAMENT The stalk of a stamen, which suports the anther.

FLORET A small flower that forms part of a composite flower, or flower head.

GERMINATION When a seed begins to sprout and grow.

GYMNOSPERM A plant whose seeds do not develop inside an ovary. Most gymnosperms are coniferous trees.

HARDY Being able to withstand extremes of temperature, such as cold and frost.

MONOCOT A plant whose seeds have a single cotyledon (seed-leaf). The leaves of a monocot, or monocotyledon, usually have parallel veins.

MULTICELLULAR Made up of more than one cell.

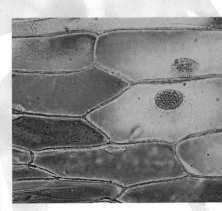

Microscopic view of typical plant cells

NECTAR A naturally occurring sweet liquid found in the glands of many flowers.

OVARY A female reproductive organ, which encloses fertilized seeds.

OVULE A collection of female cells that form a seed after they have been fertilized by pollen.

PAPPUS A ring or parachute of very fine hair that grows above a seed and helps it to be dispersed by the wind.

PARACHUTE Any structure that aids the spread of seeds by the wind, such as a pappus.

PARASITE An organism that lives in or on another organism, or host, from which it takes food and energy without giving anything back in return.

PERENNIAL A plant that lasts or flowers for more than two years.

PERIANTH The part of a flower made up of the calyx and the corolla together.

PETAL A leafy flap in a flower, often brightly coloured to attract animal pollinators.

Strawberry, a dicot plant

PHLOEM A system of cells that carries nutrients throughout a plant.

PHOTOSYNTHESIS The process by which plants generate their own food, occurring when a green pigment called chlorophyll reacts with sunlight, carbon dioxide, and water to make carbohydrates, water, and oxygen.

PIGMENT A coloured chemical used by plants to collect light. One pigment, chlorophyll, makes plants look green.

PLANTLET A young plant, which is sometimes attached to its parent.

PLUMULE The embryo shoot in a seed.

POLLEN Microscopic grains containing male sex cells. Pollen is produced by the anthers of flowers.

POLLINATION The process by which pollen is carried from one flower to another. The male pollen fertilizes the female ovule and creates a seed. Insects and animals often carry pollen between flowering plants, or it can be blown by the wind.

RECEPTACLE The part of a plant that contains the flower, or in flowerless plants, the reproductive organs or spores.

RHIZOME A creeping underground stem. Rhizomes often sprout leaves as they push their way through the ground.

ROOT The part of a plant that anchors it to a solid surface, such as soil, and absorbs water and nutrients.

RUNNER A stem that produces new plants by growing across the ground and sprouting roots.

Bamboo, a monocot plant

Poppy seeds scattered by the wind

SEED A tough structure used by plants to reproduce. A seed contains a young plant, or embryo, together with all the food reserves it needs to start life on its own.

SEPAL A leafy flap that protects a flower while it is still a bud. Sepals often fall off when the flower opens.

SHOOT The parts of a plant above ground, including its stems, leaves, and flowers.

SPADIX A fleshy spike of flowers.

SPATHE A leaf-like hood that partly encloses a flowerhead.

SPECIES A group of plants, or other living things, that look similar, and that normally breed together in the wild.

SPORE A single-celled reproductive unit of some organisms.

SPUR A flowering or fruit-bearing branch that shoots out from an existing plant.

STAMEN The pollen-producing part of a flower, consisting of a filament and an anther.

STARCH The main food type stored in a plant. Chemically known as a carbohydrate, this food contains vital energy reserves.

STEM The part of a plant that carries the leaves. Also known as a stalk, the stem transports water and food from the roots to the rest of the plant.

STIGMA The structure in a flower that receives pollen during pollination.

STOMA An opening through which gases enter and leave the green part of a plant.

STYLE The stalk-like structure in a flower that connects the stigma with the ovary.

TAPROOT A main root growing down.

TENDER A plant that is sensitive to the cold.

TENDRIL A thread-like part of a plant that grows outwards and wraps around nearby objects, helping the plant to stay upright.

TEPAL A flap around a flower that performs the functions of both sepal and petal.

TESTA A hard shell or coating around a seed.

Variegated ivy leaf

TRANSPIRATION The movement of water through a plant. Water is taken up by the roots, and it evaporates through pores in the leaves.

TUBER A swelling or lump that forms in a root or stem and usually contains valuable food reserves for the rest of the plant. A potato is a tuber.

UMBEL An umbrella-shaped flowerhead.

VARIEGATED Streaked or mottled, with contrasting colours. In plants, variegated leaves are caused by differences in the pigments across the leaf.

VEGETATION The plants found in a particular habitat, or environment.

WHORL A collection of leaves, sepals, or petals growing in a circle around a plant stem.

XYLEM A system of cells that carries water through a plant. In shrubs and trees, toughened xylem cells form wood.

ZYGOTE A fertilized egg.

Index

Acknowledgements

Dorling Kindersley would like to thank:
Brinsley Burbidge, Valerie Whalley, John Lonsdale, Milan Swaderlig, Andrew McRobb, Marilyn Ward, and Pat Griggs of the Royal Botanic Gardens, Kew. Arthur Chater at the Natural History Museum.
David Burnie for consultancy.
Dave King for special photography pp.8–9, and Peter Radcliffe p.63.
Fred Ford and Mike Pilley at Radius for artwork.
Sarah Pond and Will Giles for illustrations pp.12–13, 17, 38.

Proofreading: Sarah Owens.
Wallchart: Peter Radcliffe, Steve Setford
Clipart CD: Jo Little, Lisa Stock, Claire Watts, Jessamy Wood

Picture credits
The publisher would like to thank the following for their kind permission to reproduce their photographs:

(Key: a-above; b-below/bottom; c-centre; f-far; l-left; r-right; t-top)

A-Z Botanical: 55c; Heather Angel/ Biofotos: 43c; 49cl; V. Angel/Daily Telegraph Colour Library: 39bc; Australian High Commission: 24tr; 57tr; A.N.T./NHPA: 25cr; J. and M. Bain/NHPA: 11bl; G.I. Bernard/Oxford Scientific Films: 7tl; 46br; G.I. Bernard/NHPA: 15tr; 18cr; 36c; 40cr; Deni Bown/Oxford Scientific Films: 64bc; Bridgeman Art Library: 55cb; 58br; Brinsley Burbidge/Royal Botanic Gardens, Kew: 50bc; 58c; M.Z. Capell/ ZEFA: 10tr; James H. Carmichael/ NHPA: 53br; Gene Cox/Science Photo Library: 7c; Stephen Dalton/NHPA: 19tr; 22cl; 30tl; 36tr; 40cl; P. Dayanandan/Science Photo Library: 9tl; Jack Dermid/Oxford Scientific Films: 32br; Dr. Dransfield/Royal Botanic Gardens, Kew: 45 ; Mary Evans Picture Library: 44 tl; 46bl; 48cl; 56tl, tr; 60tr; 61 br; 62tc; Patrick Fagot/ NHPA: 71bl; Robert Francis/South American Pictures: 54tl; Linda Gamlin: 27cr; 29bc; Brian Hawkes/ NHPA: 23tl; Hulton Picture Library: 42tl; E.A. Janes/NHPA: 28bl; 68br; Peter Lillie/Oxford Scientific Films: 65b, 67b; Patrick Lynch/Science Photo Library: 6tc; 8br; Mansell Collection: 8bl; 59bc; Marion Morrison/South American Pictures: 59c; Peter Newark's Western Americana: 52br; Oxford Scientific Films: 66tl; Brian M. Rogers/ Biofotos: 46bc; Royal Botanic Gardens, Kew: 16tl; 43tl; 60c; 61c; John Shaw/ NHPA: 9tl; 64tl, br; Survival Anglia: 7tl; Silvestris Fotoservice/FLPA: 65tl; John Walsh/Science Photo Library: 15tl; M.I. Walker/NHPA: 70tr; J. Watkins/Frank Lane Picture Agency: 50bl; Alan Williams: 68tr; Rogers Wilmshurst/Frank Lane: 26tr; David Woodfall/NHPA: 68c; Steven Wooster: 69tr

Wallchart:
Corbis: Visuals Unlimited 1cra (chloroplasts)

Jacket:
Front: image100/Corbis: b; all other images: DK Images
Back (all images): DK Images

Every effort has been made to trace the copyright holders. Dorling Kindersley apologises for any unintentional omissions and would be pleased, in such cases, to add an acknowledgement in future editions.

All other images © Dorling Kindersley For further information see: www.dkimages.com